ROGER STEVENSON
1987

ROGER STEVENSON
1987

BUILDING SOLAR

BUILDING SOLAR

HOW THE PROFESSIONAL BUILDER IS MAKING SOLAR CONSTRUCTION WORK

Karen Muller Wells

 VAN NOSTRAND REINHOLD COMPANY

Copyright © 1984 by Van Nostrand Reinhold Company Inc.

Library of Congress Catalog Card Number: 83-21744
ISBN: 0-442-29268-6

Manufactured in the United States of America

Published by Van Nostrand Reinhold Company Inc.
135 West 50th Street
New York, New York 10020

Van Nostrand Reinhold Company Limited
Molly Millars Lane
Wokingham, Berkshire RG11 2PY, England

Van Nostrand Reinhold
480 Latrobe Street
Melbourne, Victoria 3000, Australia

Macmillan of Canada
Division of Gage Publishing Limited
164 Commander Boulevard
Agincourt, Ontario MIS 3C7, Canada

15 14 13 12 11 10 9 8 7 6 5 4 3 2

Library of Congress Cataloging in Publication Data

Wells, Karen Muller.
   Building solar.

   Includes index.
   1. Solar houses--Design and construction. I. Title.
TH7414.W44   1983   690'.869   83-21744
ISBN 0-442-29268-6

CONTENTS

FOREWORD

The concept of harnessing solar energy has been, and continues to be, the single most challenging and adventuresome aspect of energy conservation in home building.

The theory of solar energy application has been known for centuries. Earlier civilizations applied it with skill. But the availability of abundant, low-priced fossil fuels virtually eliminated use of, and interest in, solar energy applications in building for most of this century.

But with the rapid run-up of energy costs in the last decade, interest has refocused on solar energy. The challenge for builders today is to put solar energy to work in a practical and economical way that can be readily sold to buyers

And that is what this book, BUILDING SOLAR, is all about—the real-world efforts of American builders to harness solar energy for new housing in today's economy.

Much of the material published here originally appeared in *Professional Builder* magazine,

researched, reported, and written for the magazine by Karen Muller Wells. As an associate editor for *Professional Builder*, Ms. Wells was for several years the magazine's specialist on matters of energy in building.

In this book she has organized, rewritten, and added to the original material published in *Professional Builder*. The result is a practical handbook for builders on the use of solar energy.

Because of the changing nature of building technology, no one book can provide all the answers on the subject of solar energy application in home building. But this book pulls together a wealth of information on what can and cannot be done in today's real building economy. It is, we believe, a "must" for the successful builder's reading and reference library.

DAVID E. LINK
Editorial Director
Professional Builder

ACKNOWLEDGMENTS

This book is dedicated to those builders who accepted the challenges of incorporating solar principles into their building practices. It is dedicated to those who tried and failed, to those who tried and succeeded, and mostly to those with the perseverance to keep on trying.

Many thanks to Roy L. Diez, editor of *Professional Builder* magazine, who acted as a consultant on this book. I appreciate his editorial help and direction in putting the book together. I also thank David E. Link, editorial director and associate publisher of *Professional Builder*, for suggesting the genesis of this project. Much of the material appeared in whole or in part on the pages of *Professional Builder*. I also commend my husband Bill for his encouragement in completing the manuscript.

And many thanks to those builders, designers, and architects who shared their experiences and lessons with me. They made this book possible.

KAREN MULLER WELLS
Chicago, Illinois

INTRODUCTION

The benefits of solar energy as an energy source have been known and proven for decades. Solar water heaters were commonly used in California and Florida prior to World War II. By the early 1950s, Miami alone had about 50,000 installations.

A federal study commissioned by the Truman administration in the early 1950s concluded that "economical solar energy could be developed over five years if the country put sufficient resources into the effort," stated an article in the New York Times. But, unfortunately, "Oil was then so cheap and plentiful that the finding was shelved as irrelevant." And architecture adapted itself to an era of cheap energy.

Energy costs have now become the impetus for solar development. Since the early 1970s, monthly energy costs have escalated to the point where they are often running neck-in-neck with the mortgage payments and driving up the real cost of owning a home—and, subsequently, challenging the affordability of the American dream.

Interest in solar energy has followed the increasing concern about high home-heating bills. Each step up the inflationary energy ladder brings buyers and builders closer to the solar alternative.

The energy crisis, in a few short years, revolutionized politics and the automobile industry. But builders are now realizing that those same energy concerns are also changing the way Americans seek and purchase new homes. Energy efficiency is an important issue in the minds of prospective buyers. But it is not just a passive concern. Many are actively looking for a more energy-efficient house as a result of the high cost of energy. Consumers are now demanding energy efficiency in the homes they buy. As a result, interest in solar energy is increasing at a rapid pace.

It has been estimated that six to eight times the energy required to heat the average building in the United States radiates down on that building from the sun each year. The challenge is to harness that energy to its greatest use.

Studies, research, demonstration grants, and computer simulations all have been important in the development of solar energy in the building industry. But most important has been the practical experience of those in the field. The most successful solar projects have been developed by builders who incorporated technical principles, ingenuity, and interest into their own marketable solar plans.

"It's something that I've always wanted to try my hand at," one builder reflected on his first solar construction experience. He was not armed with scientific data, computer input, and a government grant. He possessed a stronger incentive. He had the mind of an innovator and an entrepreneur. He knew that his own experience was the best education that he could find. And he foresaw that in the coming years, he would have something very valuable: hands-on experience.

And that is what this book is all about: the nuts-and-bolts experience in solar construction of builders across the country. In the past few years, some of the rough edges of solar construction have been sanded down. A lot of lessons were learned. In the coming years, the state of the art will become even more refined as solar systems become even more efficient and economical. Solar energy systems, however, cannot be refined without hands-on builder experience.

Builders must be concerned with energy-efficient construction techniques. But they must also be very much aware of marketability. It is a delicate balance. And this balance is vital to the development of solar energy in the building industry.

This book is not meant to be a theoretical textbook. It was written for professional builders and others actively interested in solar energy construction.

BUILDING SOLAR

Solar buildings are designed to maximize use of a virtually untapped energy source: the sun. Buildings can utilize the sun's rays mechanically or passively through the structure itself.

1

SYSTEMS PRIMER

A solar house or building can incorporate active solar mechanical equipment or passive solar design principles or both. In this chapter, the basic characteristics of both passive and active solar systems are discussed, including system features and designs and equipment for residential and small commercial applications.

But first, it should be noted that a key to the success of any solar application is the overall level of energy-efficient construction. This means the ability of the structure to reduce heat loss. Energy savers such as adequate insulation, multiple-glazed windows, caulking, weatherstripping, insulated doors, and others are vital components in any solar system. The less heat lost, the greater contribution the sun can make in heating the structure. In an energy-conserving house, collected solar heat can be retained for optimum efficiency. Once heat loss has been minimized, the type of solar system—active or passive—can be considered.

Active solar systems for space heat or domestic hot water are not as complicated as they initially appear. Basically, active solar systems heat a structure mechanically using components common in conventional heating systems, such as ducts, tanks, and air distributors. Because most solar systems do not supply 100 percent of the home's heating needs, solar systems most often work in conjunction with a conventional heating, ventilation, and air conditioning (HVAC) system, as is the case with a solar-assisted heat pump or water heater. Conventional systems provide backup, supplemental heat when the sun is not shining and solar heat storage may be depleted.

In most active solar systems, the most visible component of the system is the solar collectors, typically mounted on the roof of the house or adjacent structure. The most common type of active solar system is based on flat-plate collectors, rectangular box-type units. In these systems, solar radia-

FLAT-PLATE SOLAR COLLECTOR

A typical flat-plate collector consists of several layers: a transparent cover, an absorber plate usually painted or coated black, channels or tubes through which a liquid or air passes to be heated, and an insulated structure to contain these elements. The collectors, installed on a south-facing roof, are connected by pipes or ducts to heat distribution equipment or storage, depending on the immediate need for the solar heat. A liquid-type flat-plate collector is shown. SOURCE: U.S. Department of Housing and Urban Development.

3

tion passes through a transparent cover consisting of glass or other high-emittance material. The radiation is absorbed by a black-painted or coated plate, typically made of sheet metal. The solar heat is transferred to air or liquid which passes through channels in the collector plate. The air or liquid then is transported through ducts or pipes to a heat exchanger for distribution of the heat or hot water throughout the house, if needed immediately, or to a storage area for later use.

Active solar collectors require unobstructed space on the roof of the house or on an adjacent structure which faces within 20 degrees of due south for maximum efficiency. The collector area should not be shaded by adjacent buildings or vegetation. Also, collectors should be installed with at least a 30 degree angle to the sun so that radiation

will not be reflected away from the collector instead of being absorbed. The optimum collector angle for solar space heating and water heating is considered equal to the site latitude plus or minus 10 degrees.

Collectors are basically divided into two types of systems: air and liquid. In an air-based system, air is blown through roof-top collectors to be heated by the sun. The heated air is distributed through a forced-air furnace to supply heat directly to the house if needed. When the house reaches the thermostat setting, the solar-heated air is transported through ducts into a storage bin which is usually filled with rocks or water. Heat is stored in the bin or tank until needed at night or on overcast days. Liquid systems work on the same principle, except that a liquid, typically an antifreeze solution, is used as the heat medium.

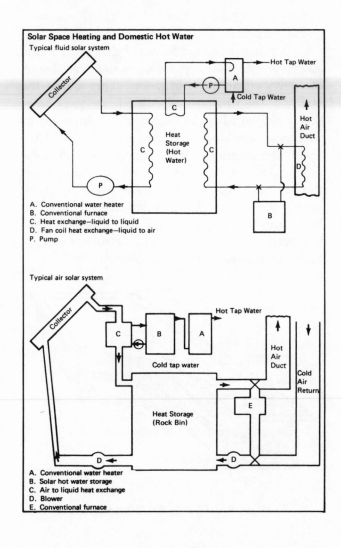

Two drawings show how typical liquid and air-type solar systems operate to supply space heat and hot water in residential applications. The liquid-type systems commonly use water tanks for storage of solar heat. Air-type systems typically utilize rock storage bins. Most systems for space heat and hot water will be based on a variation of these simple plans. SOURCE: Federal Energy Administration.

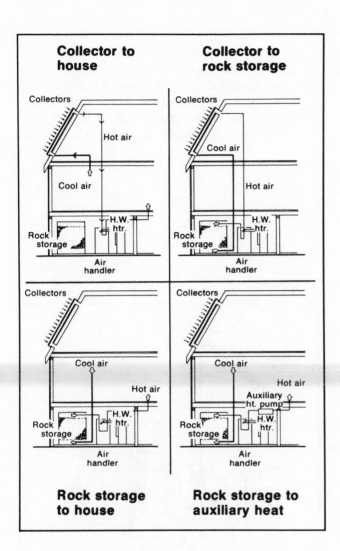

Collector to house

Collector to rock storage

Rock storage to house

Rock storage to auxiliary heat

The schematic illustrates how a basic air-type solar system works. The system will provide a portion of the house's heat and hot water requirements depending on location, house style, and size. Air, heated by the sun, moves from the collectors to the air-handling unit to heat the house and hot water. When the temperature in the house reaches the desired thermostat setting, excess heat moves to the storage area where rocks absorb the heat. The stored solar heat can be used at night and on cloudy days. For extended periods of cold and cloudy weather, a furnace or heat pump is needed to provide auxiliary heat.

Both air- and liquid-type systems have been demonstrated in homes and small commercial structures across the United States. Both have advantages and disadvantages. Air systems are mostly used in space-heating applications. Liquid systems are used in both space-heating and water-heating applications. Examples of various systems and actual installations are featured throughout this book, including schematic drawings to help show how these systems operate.

In the future, it is expected that photovoltaic solar systems, which directly convert sunlight into electricity, may also prove to be an effective and efficient way of heating and cooling buildings. But while significant progress in increasing efficiency and reducing per-kilowatt cost has been made, cost-efficient applications of photovoltaic systems are still primarily in the research and development stage.

The number of collectors needed in a solar installation depends on a number of factors. The type of system determines how many collectors are needed, whether the system is expected to supply space heat, cooling, or water heating, and what percentage of the heating or cooling requirements the sun is expected to contribute. A system that supplies both space heating and water heating, for example, typically requires more collector area than a system that only supplies water heating.

The climate and region of the country also determine the amount of expected sunlight and the heating requirements of the house. More collectors are needed in cloudy or cold areas. In addition, the size of the house and the number of occupants af-

Active Solar Water Heating Systems

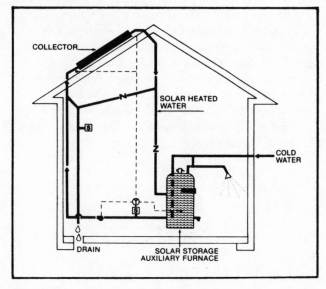

Open Loop

Open Loop *Domestic water is heated directly through collectors and stored in a tank for direct use. Minor freezing problems at night are prevented by letting the water in the system drain down when the pump shuts off.* SOURCE: U.S. Department of Housing and Urban Development.

Closed Loop

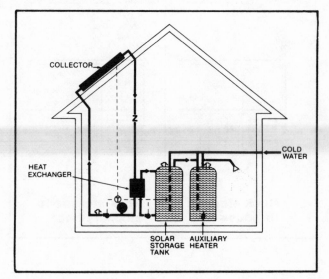

Closed Loop *Water is heated by the sun indirectly through use of solar-heated antifreeze solution which passes through a heat exchanger. Recommended for climates where freezing may occur.* SOURCE: U.S. Department of Housing and Urban Development.

fect the number of solar collectors needed to supply a certain percentage of the house's heating requirements. And the efficiency of the solar system itself may determine how many collectors are needed. A system that absorbs, retains, transports, and stores solar heat more efficiently requires far fewer collectors than a poorly designed system. Efficiency depends on the manufacturer, installer, and specific system.

Another major component of active solar systems is storage of excess solar heat for use at night, on overcast days, or in extremely cold conditions. In liquid collector systems, solar heat is typically stored in large, insulated water tanks located under the house, in the basement or garage, constructed of metal or concrete.

In air-type collector systems, rock storage is considered the most effective way of storing heat. Some systems also use phase-change chemicals to store excess heat. The chemicals, comprised of eutectic salts, melt when exposed to very warm air, absorbing the heat. When heat is needed, the chemicals cool and resolidify, releasing the heat to the surrounding air. These chemicals are typically used in solar installations in tube-like structures, which also may be surrounded by an insulated tank or bin.

The most popular type of solar collector system has been the liquid-type. Its major advantage is its effectiveness in domestic solar water heating installations, which is the most widespread application of active solar energy in residential structures.

Water heating comprises about 15 percent of a home's heating requirements.

There are three basic types of liquid-type solar water heating systems. An *open-loop system* heats the domestic water directly in the collectors. A *closed-loop system* utilizes a heat-transfer fluid that passes through a heat exchanger in a water heater tank. Closed-loop systems are recommended for cold climates where freezing may occur. A *thermosyphoning water heating system* (sometimes considered a passive solar system) allows the natural circulation of water through the collector. Water warmed in the collector rises to a storage tank in the attic of the house. Cooler water in the tank flows to the bottom of the collector. Heated water is supplied directly through an open-loop system for domestic uses.

In general, liquid-type systems are more efficient in transporting the solar-heated medium from the roof collectors to storage areas through small pipes, as opposed to large ducts used in air-type collector systems. The storage of solar heat in liquid-type systems also requires less space than in air-type systems—an important consideration in applications where space is tight, such as small homes, attached townhomes, and solar retrofit projects.

Liquid-type systems, however, can cause problems with leaks, freezing, and corrosion, although most problems can be eliminated through the use of a quality system from a reliable manufacturer and through installation by an experienced solar or HVAC contractor or plumber.

Air-type collector systems are most efficient for space-heating applications because solar heat can be ducted directly from the collectors to the living space, if required by the thermostat. In liquid-type systems for space heating, some efficiency is lost through the transfer of heat from the liquid to a forced-air furnace through use of a heat exchanger. Air systems, on the other hand, are not typically efficient in water-heating applications. Also, transportation of heat from collectors to storage in air-type systems requires large insulated ducts, rather than small pipes used in liquid systems. Note the list of system characteristics in the chart on this page, which compares the advantages and disadvantages of each system.

PROS AND CONS

Solar System	Advantages	Disadvantages
Air	No freezing problems. Few leaks with little consequence. Can be used to directly heat the house with no temperature losses due to heat exchangers when the system is used in a space heating application. No boiling or pressure problems.	Can only be used to heat homes, not economically adapted to cooling applications. Large air ducts needed. Larger storage area needed for rocks. Heat exchangers needed if system is used to heat water.
Liquid (or Water)	Holds and transfers heat well. Water can be used as storage medium. Can be used for space heating, cooling, and water heating applications. Compact storage and small conduits.	Leaking, freezing, and corrosion can be problems. Corrosion inhibitors needed in water when using steel or aluminum. Noncorrosive and nonelectrolytic liquids are not recommended due to toxicity and flammability. To prevent freezing, a separate collector loop with an antifreeze liquid and a heat exchanger, or a drain-down system, are required in cold climates. In warm regions, electric warmers can be used.

Source: Adapted from *Buying Solar* compiled by the Federal Energy Administration.

A good passive solar home begins with energy efficiency. As south-facing glass and thermal storage mass are added, the conventional heating load decreases and the contribution of passive solar heat increases, as shown in the chart.
SOURCE: U.S. Department of Housing and Urban Development.

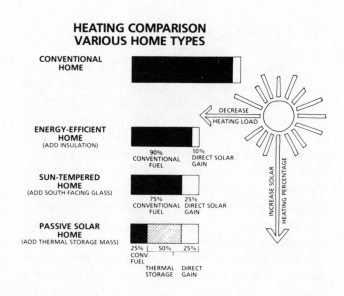

HEATING COMPARISON VARIOUS HOME TYPES

No one type of collection system is perfect for every application. Much depends on heating requirements, type of installation, storage capabilities, and climate. Efficiency of the system is the most important consideration, not only in system performance, but also in the price of the system. The system that delivers the most heat for the dollar will prove to be the most efficient, and not necessarily the most expensive initially. As in selecting any building materials, appliances, or mechanical equipment, careful research is required to select the best system for a particular installation, whether in a large custom home or a tract of solar single-family units.

In designing a solar house, several aspects of the mechanical system should be considered and discussed with the architect, engineer, and appropriate subcontractors including HVAC installers, plumbers, roofers, and carpenters. First, adequate south-facing space must be provided on the roof for the solar collectors. The roof structure itself must be able to support the added weight of the solar collectors. Aesthetically, the collector system should be integrated into the architecture of the house, following the slope and lines of the roof, rather than being tacked on at an odd angle as a potential eyesore.

Inside the house, space must be allocated for the piping or ductwork to transport the solar-heated liquid or air to the heat exchanger, air-handling equipment, or storage. An insulated tank or storage bin must be specified in the basement, garage, or under the house to store excess solar heat for later use.

One solar architect mentioned that the most common mistake among builders who try solar for the first time is that they do not adequately check

out a variety of products and systems. A lower cost system may not be a better buy; a more expensive system may not provide the most efficiency.

But the architect noted that the biggest mistake that builders make concerning solar construction is that they do not even consider building solar at all. Based on misconceptions and problems heard about early installations, builders assume that solar is not for them. Of course, there are regional differences in performance, but solar projects have been successful in every region of the country. Moreover, many of the problems encountered by builders in the early 1970s have been eliminated through improved solar system design by manufacturers, information supplied through demonstration programs and by hands-on experience of builders themselves.

Most experienced solar builders, architects, and engineers agree that the simpler the solar system, the better. Complex systems have a tendency to require more extensive and expensive maintenance.

One of the simplest ways to use the sun in heating a home or small commercial space is passive solar heating. It requires no moving parts in most systems; and most builders and buyers consider it maintenance-free.

A passive solar system does not rely on mechanical equipment as used in active solar systems. Passive solar systems use the structure of the house itself as the solar collector, using the same collection principles in active solar systems. In a passive solar system, south-facing glazed areas and the insulated house serve as the solar collector.

Passive solar construction is not new. It is nothing more than designing homes to be responsive to the regional climate or environment. The principles were developed and utilized hundreds of years ago. Regional architecture notes these differences. Long overhangs, sun porches, salt-box roof slopes, and adobe building materials all reflect the

ways buildings responded to various climates in the days before inexpensive and readily available heating fuel. The adoption of passive solar design is partly based on a return to these historic architectural principles. These houses took advantage of the natural energy saving elements found inherently on the building site.

The purpose of passive solar design is to take the maximum advantage of the house design, orientation, and air flow to naturally heat and cool a house, reducing its reliance on conventionally

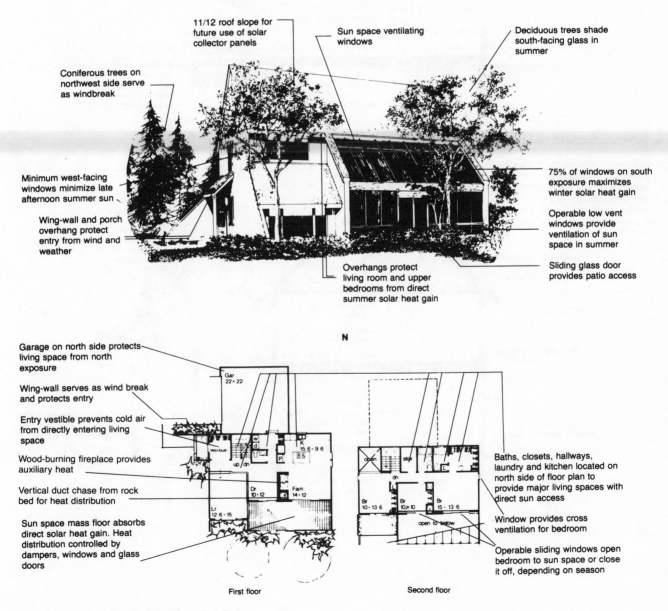

11/12 roof slope for future use of solar collector panels

Sun space ventilating windows

Deciduous trees shade south-facing glass in summer

Coniferous trees on northwest side serve as windbreak

Minimum west-facing windows minimize late afternoon summer sun

Wing-wall and porch overhang protect entry from wind and weather

75% of windows on south exposure maximizes winter solar heat gain

Operable low vent windows provide ventilation of sun space in summer

Overhangs protect living room and upper bedrooms from direct summer solar heat gain

Sliding glass door provides patio access

N

Garage on north side protects living space from north exposure

Wing-wall serves as wind break and protects entry

Entry vestibule prevents cold air from directly entering living space

Wood-burning fireplace provides auxiliary heat

Vertical duct chase from rock bed for heat distribution

Sun space mass floor absorbs direct solar heat gain. Heat distribution controlled by dampers, windows and glass doors

Baths, closets, hallways, laundry and kitchen located on north side of floor plan to provide major living spaces with direct sun access

Window provides cross ventilation for bedroom

Operable sliding windows open bedroom to sun space or close it off, depending on season

First floor

Second floor

DRAWINGS: John D. Bloodgood A.I.A.

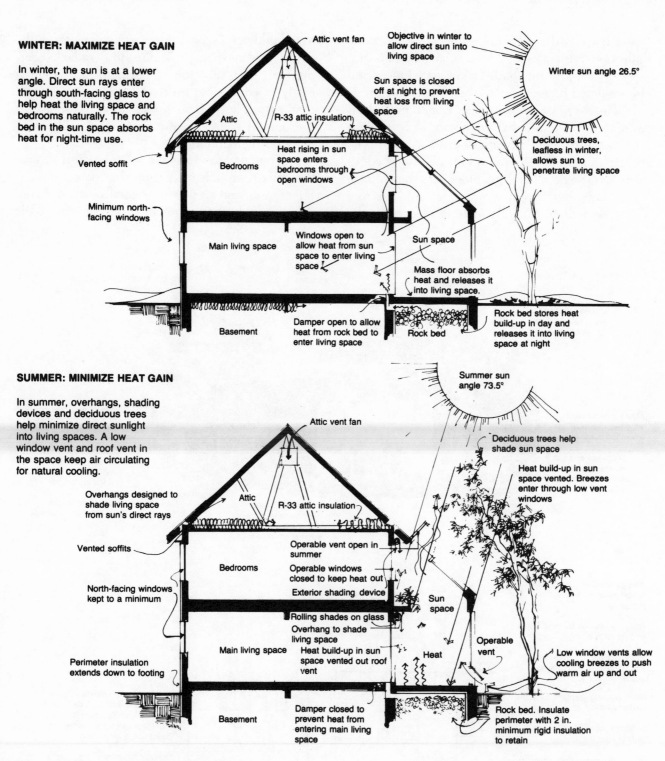

WINTER: MAXIMIZE HEAT GAIN

In winter, the sun is at a lower angle. Direct sun rays enter through south-facing glass to help heat the living space and bedrooms naturally. The rock bed in the sun space absorbs heat for night-time use.

Attic vent fan

Objective in winter to allow direct sun into living space

Winter sun angle 26.5°

Sun space is closed off at night to prevent heat loss from living space

R-33 attic insulation

Attic

Vented soffit

Deciduous trees, leafless in winter, allows sun to penetrate living space

Heat rising in sun space enters bedrooms through open windows

Bedrooms

Minimum north-facing windows

Main living space

Windows open to allow heat from sun space to enter living space

Sun space

Mass floor absorbs heat and releases it into living space.

Basement

Damper open to allow heat from rock bed to enter living space

Rock bed

Rock bed stores heat build-up in day and releases it into living space at night

SUMMER: MINIMIZE HEAT GAIN

In summer, overhangs, shading devices and deciduous trees help minimize direct sunlight into living spaces. A low window vent and roof vent in the space keep air circulating for natural cooling.

Summer sun angle 73.5°

Attic vent fan

Deciduous trees help shade sun space

Heat build-up in sun space vented. Breezes enter through low vent windows

Overhangs designed to shade living space from sun's direct rays

Attic

R-33 attic insulation

Vented soffits

Bedrooms

Operable vent open in summer

Operable windows closed to keep heat out

Exterior shading device

North-facing windows kept to a minimum

Sun space

Rolling shades on glass

Overhang to shade living space

Main living space

Heat build-up in sun space vented out roof vent

Heat

Operable vent

Perimeter insulation extends down to footing

Low window vents allow cooling breezes to push warm air up and out

Basement

Damper closed to prevent heat from entering main living space

Rock bed. Insulate perimeter with 2 in. minimum rigid insulation to retain

DRAWINGS: John D. Bloodgood A.I.A.

fueled heating and cooling equipment. The goal of most passive solar homes is not to entirely replace the need for conventional heating and cooling systems, but to supplement those systems and reduce the time that equipment is needed to operate in order to maintain a comfortable temperature in the home. Wood stoves also can be incorporated for supplemental heat, or a hybrid system can be used, combining active and passive solar systems.

The goal should be to maximize occupant comfort and energy savings. As one builder noted about passive solar design, "It is just a natural way of building." Most passive solar features are based on building materials and construction techniques that are familiar to builders of conventional homes. Passive solar design and construction is not dependent on one component, but on an integration of many elements including building materials, design, orientation, landscaping, and room arrangement.

As shown in the plan on the previous two pages, designed by architect John D. Bloodgood A.I.A., passive solar incorporates the structure of the house as a solar collector through means of south-facing glass. Natural heating occurs as the house absorbs available sunlight. But heat gain is only one part of passive solar design. In summer, the house increases natural ventilation and air circulation through shading devices, overhangs, and windows.

This plan was designed to show how passive solar could be accommodated in a conventional plan, familiar to any builder, built with a traditional or contemporary front elevation. The house design, floor plan, and building envelope all must act together to maximize natural heating and cooling.

The three basic components of passive solar systems generally are collection, storage, and distribution of solar heat gain in winter months and of natural ventilation in summer months. The idea behind passive solar is to incorporate the system into the house, serving as an integral element of the structure.

To identify passive solar homes for tax purposes, the Department of Energy and the Internal Revenue Service developed a set of five recognition factors for passive solar homes. The list is a definitive checklist for passive solar design. According to DOE and IRS, all five factors must be included:

1. A *solar collection area* comprised of an expanse of transparent or translucent material located on the side of the structure which faces within 30 degrees of due south.

2. An *absorber* consisting of a hard surface exposed to the sun's rays in the solar collection area. The absorber converts the solar radiation into heat and transfers that heat to the storage mass.

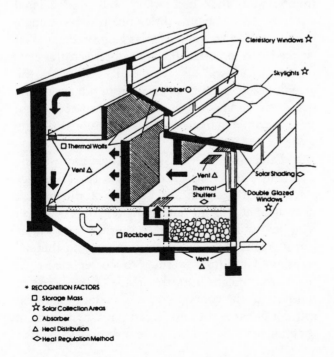

Clerestory Windows ☆
Skylights ☆
Absorber ○
Thermal Walls □
Vent △
Vent △
Solar Shading ◇
Thermal Shutters
Double Glazed Windows ☆
Rockbed □
Vent △

* RECOGNITION FACTORS
□ Storage Mass
☆ Solar Collection Areas
○ Absorber
△ Heat Distribution
◇ Heat Regulation Method

To define a passive solar house for proposed tax credit purposes, the Department of Energy and the Internal Revenue Service developed five basic recognition factors. To qualify for the proposed credits, a passive solar house must include all five factors: storage mass, solar collection areas, absorber, and heat distribution and heat regulation methods. Examples are shown in the illustration. SOURCE: U.S. Department of Energy.

3. A *storage mass* comprised of a dense, heavy material to receive and hold heat from the absorber and later release the heat to the home's interior spaces. Size and exposure of the mass to the sun must be adequate to provide sufficient heat for the home, and the mass must be located properly for heat distribution.

4. A *heat distribution method* to release the heat from the storage mass to the living areas of the house.

5. *Heat regulation devices* including shades and vents to control heat build-up in the collection area in hot summer months. These devices also include insulation to control heat loss from the interior of the structure.

All passive solar homes will not necessarily include all five recognition factors, depending on the extent of desired energy savings. A passive solar house should be designed primarily for energy savings and occupant comfort. Performance, not a checklist of elements, is what counts.

Most builders are already capable of producing well-designed, passive solar homes, said Joseph Sherman, director of solar energy programs at the Department of Housing and Urban Development. Through his experience in directing two passive solar demonstration programs under HUD, Sherman said that builders should not be scared off by the concept of passive solar. Common sense, attention to detail, and familiarity with passive solar design principles are all it takes to build a good passive solar home, he said. And as most HUD experts stress, the best passive solar designs are kept simple.

The three most common passive solar heating methods are direct, indirect, and isolated heat gain. Each of these methods can be used separately in a home, but for maximum performance, all can be incorporated to work together.

Very simply, a *direct gain* system allows the sun's rays to penetrate the living space through south-facing windows to heat the living spaces directly. A direct gain system is the most economical passive solar element to incorporate. It utilizes a simple physical law of air-to-air heat transfer. The principle is as simple as how a car parked in the sunlight will collect solar radiation and become warm inside, even in winter. The sun's heat is absorbed. By orienting a house's glazed areas to the south, windows are transformed from a source of heat loss into a source of heat gain.

A passive solar system based on *indirect solar heat gain* does not allow the sun's rays to enter the primary living spaces, as in a direct gain system. Instead, heat gain is stored in thermal storage mass, such as a trombe (thermal mass) wall. Thermal mass walls are comprised of any heavy absorbent materials such as masonry, concrete, rock, and clay tile. The darker the color, the greater the solar absorbency. Large barrels or tubes of water can also be used to absorb solar heat. Most recently, "synthetic" thermal mass is available through use of phase-change chemicals that melt as they absorb heat and crystalize as they cool to release the heat to the surrounding air. A trombe wall, typically constructed of filled concrete block painted black, is glazed on the exterior with a two-to-four-inch air space between the wall and the glazing. A masonry fireplace that is glazed on the exterior can also be incorporated as a thermal storage wall.

In an *isolated heat gain system*, solar heat is collected in a separate space such as a greenhouse or atrium. In this type of system, sunlight does not directly enter living spaces, but is collected in a separate space and stored in thermal mass such as a trombe wall, rock bed, water wall, or insulated concrete slab. The only difference between using a trombe wall in an indirect solar gain system and an isolated system is that the space between the glazing and the wall is increased. Although the greenhouse or atrium is cut off from primary living space, by sliding glass doors for instance, these areas are often marketed also as extensions of living space.

Direct use of the sun through south-facing glazed areas in living spaces or an isolated sunspace can provide a significant portion of the house's heating requirements during the day. But whatever heat has not been absorbed by thermal mass will be lost at night through convection, or the thermal transfer of air from warmer to cooler areas. At night, that means from the inside of the house or sunspace to the cool outdoors. To retain solar heat gain for use at night or overcast days, some form of thermal mass is needed to absorb and store that

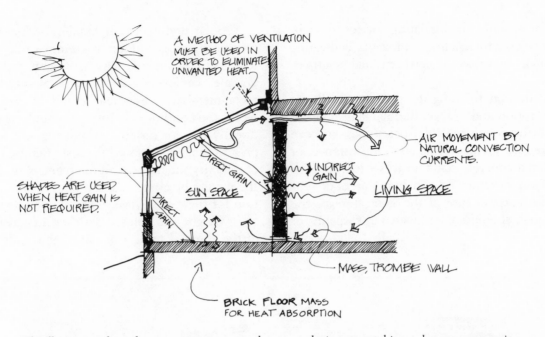

A METHOD OF VENTILATION MUST BE USED IN ORDER TO ELIMINATE UNWANTED HEAT.

AIR MOVEMENT BY NATURAL CONVECTION CURRENTS.

SHADES ARE USED WHEN HEAT GAIN IS NOT REQUIRED.

DIRECT GAIN

DIRECT GAIN

SUN SPACE

INDIRECT GAIN

LIVING SPACE

MASS, TROMBE WALL

BRICK FLOOR MASS FOR HEAT ABSORPTION

The illustration shows how a sunspace or greenhouse can be incorporated into a house or non-residential structure for passive solar heating. A vented trombe wall was included to store heat gain and circulate it throughout living spaces by means of natural convection. SOURCE: John D. Bloodgood A.I.A.

heat. Thermal mass can also help prevent overheating or wide temperature swings by absorbing excess heat during the day for use at night.

Thermal mass works on a convection principle by releasing the heat as the surrounding area becomes cooler, keeping living spaces or sunspace warm even at night. Where a trombe wall (or large masonry wall) is used, heat is naturally conducted from the sun-warmed side of the wall to the cooler side, thereby heating the interior of the house. It is a simple heat transfer. Radiant heating occurs as long as the brick is warmer than the interior air. The masonry exposed to the direct radiation of the sun acts as a heat transfer mechanism as well as a storage medium. There is, however, a time lag for the heat to penetrate the masonry wall and transmit the heat to the interior. Vents can help speed up the process of heating interior space with passive solar. Using a *vented* trombe wall, heat distribution to the interior is aided by natural convection. The heat flows through vents into the living space and cool air is routed to the sunspace where it is warmed, and a circular air flow is created. By strict definition, passive solar homes use construction

techniques rather than mechanical equipment to aid in naturally heating and cooling the house. But if it is useful, a fan or pump could help increase efficiency of the home. A ceiling fan, for instance, can help recirculate heat and reduce the effects of heat stratification in rooms with high ceilings.

At night, vents should be closed to avoid a reversal of the convection process. But even when the vents are closed, the brick wall will continue to radiate heat to the interior spaces. Insulating curtains or shutters over glazed areas at night are recommended in northern climates to get the full benefits from the passive solar heat gain by reducing nighttime heat loss.

Although a double or triple glazed south-facing window typically gains more heat than it loses, insulating shutters, curtains, and window quilts are recommended in some climates to maximize use of solar heat, minimize heat loss, and reduce temperature fluctuations inside the house. The net heat gain can be increased substantially using these devices. They help the house hold onto that gained heat. They are recommended to be most critical in a direct-gain application and in northern climates. The insulating devices, though, can also be used for shading to prevent overheating in summer months in northern *and* southern climates.

In addition to using thermal mass walls for heat absorption and storage, thermal mass floors or rock bed storage can be used. Rock storage bins can be covered with a quarry-tile floor, for instance, or an insulated concrete slab four to six inches thick can be used to retain heat in living areas or sunspace. To optimize use of the floor storage, the thermal mass should not be covered by carpeting or rugs.

Solar architect and builder Rodney Wright recommended to builders in a seminar that the critical factor in thermal mass is weight, rather than volume. For every cubic foot of glazing, Wright recommends two hundred pounds of masonry directly and continuously hit by the sun's rays. If not directly hit, for instance where rugs are scattered on a thermal mass floor, about six hundred pounds of masonry should be used to compensate, he said. If concrete block is used in a floor or wall application for thermal storage, it should be filled solid.

Wright also pointed out that, in construction of the thermal mass wall, all of the skills needed

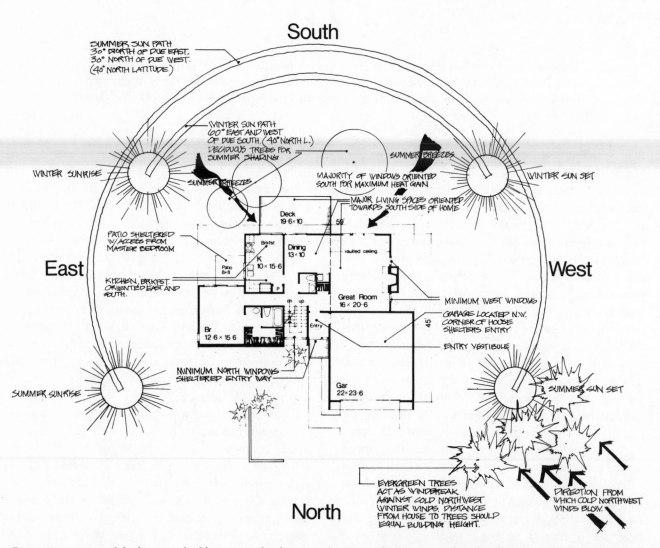

Proper orientation of the house or building can make the most of passive solar heating and cooling benefits. The plan illustrates the basics of orientation, room arrangement, and landscaping. SOURCE: John D. Bloodgood A.I.A.

exist with ordinary trades using common building materials. Another builder agreed. During construction, he said, many of his subcontractors had no idea that they were building passive solar homes.

The collection area for direct or indirect solar heat gain and the storage areas, however, are only one part of a passive solar system. The design, construction, and orientation of the entire house must be focused on energy efficiency, making the most of natural heating and cooling.

One of the most important components of passive solar systems is orientation. Natural heating cannot be optimized unless the house is oriented properly with glazed areas facing south, the garage and service areas concentrated on the north side, and landscaping and berming designed to help buffer cold winter winds. Proper orientation also helps naturally cool the house by taking advantage of prevailing breezes in summer and increasing the air flow into the house. Strategically placed trees can help shade glazed areas during hot summer months. (In the deep South, extra emphasis should be placed on outside shading devices, landscaping, and natural ventilation.)

To take optimum advantage of winter solar heat gain, living spaces should be oriented to the south. Window areas should be maximized on the south elevation and minimized on the north, east, and west exposures. In northern climates, double or triple glazing is recommended for the south-facing windows. Windows on the other exposures should be kept to a minimum and double or triple glazed. It is important to note that too much south-facing glazing can pose a problem of overheating. The amount of glazing should be balanced with the house's size and heating needs.

To reduce heat loss, closets, utility rooms, and bathrooms without windows can act as a wind buffer on the north side of the house. The garage on the north side also can act as a break from winter winds. Careful placement of the garage can also provide additional energy savings by protecting a north-facing entry. Double-door entry vestibules also should be used at the main and secondary entrances to reduce air infiltration and heat loss.

Landscaping with coniferous (evergreen) trees in the direction of prevailing winter winds forms an effective wind break. A four-to-six-foot, slotted fence can provide similar protection, optimally placed about one-and-a-half times the height of the house away from the building. Berming also can reduce air infiltration by decreasing the building's exposure and taking advantage of the earth's

Passive Solar Design

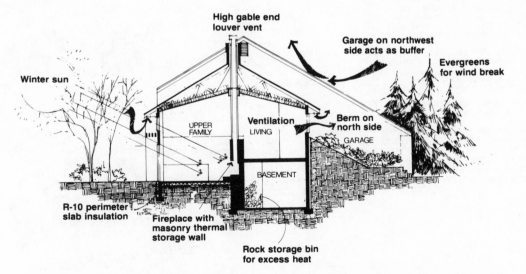

Earth berming and landscaping with evergreens on the north side of the house provide a natural buffer against cold winter winds. The garage on the northwest side also helps protect the house.
SOURCE: John D. Bloodgood A.I.A.

Single-family units

IN LAYING OUT SUBDIVISIONS CARE SHOULD BE TAKEN IN STREET ORIENTATION. EAST-WEST STREETS WILL PROVIDE MAXIMUM NUMBER OF LOTS WITH NORTH-SOUTH ORIENTATIONS, AS SHOWN IN THE PLAN AT RIGHT. AN ATTEMPT SHOULD THEN BE MADE TO ORIENT MAJOR LIVING SPACES (i.e. LIVING, FAMILY) TO THE SOUTH SIDE OF THE HOUSE, WHERE THE SUN WILL PENETRATE MOST READILY.

NOTE OUTDOOR PATIOS ON SOUTH SIDE OF HOUSE, A NATURAL EXTENSION OFF OF MAJOR LIVING SPACES. EAST PATIOS ARE AN ACCEPTABLE ALTERNATIVE.

LANDSCAPE PLANNING SHOULD TAKE INTO ACCOUNT WINDBREAKS. ALSO PRIVACY FENCES WITH LANDSCAPING WILL ENHANCE OUTDOOR DECKS AND PATIOS

NOTE ALL HOMES HAVE THEIR GARAGES ON THE NORTHWEST CORNER, GIVING ADDED PROTECTION FROM COLD WINTER WINDS.

LOCATE EVERGREENS ON NORTHWEST SIDE OF HOMES, SHADE TREES ON SOUTH SIDES.

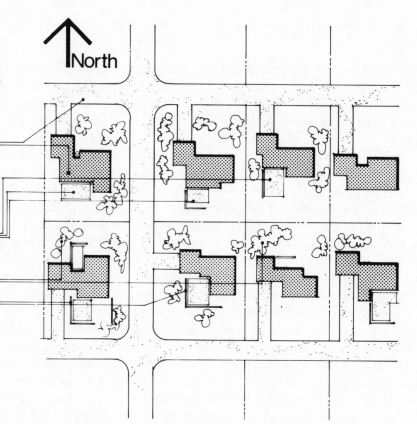

Multifamily units

EARTH BERMS WITH EVERGREENS AND PLANTING PROVIDE WIND SHELTER AND ACT ALSO AS PRIVACY FENCES OR BUFFERS.

IN A MULTIFAMILY DEVELOPMENT, AGAIN YOU WANT TO ORIENT THE UNITS NORTH-SOUTH WITH STREETS RUNNING EAST-WEST AS IN THIS PLAN.

GARAGES ARE LOCATED ON NORTH AND NORTHWEST SIDES OF UNITS

MAJOR LIVING SPACES ORIENT SOUTH WITH PATIOS

MAJOR LIVING SPACES ORIENT AND LOOK OUT ONTO COMMUNITY GREEN.

LANDSCAPING PROVIDE WINDBREAKS AND PRIVACY SCREENS BETWEEN UNITS.

LOCATE EVERGREENS ON NORTHWEST SIDE OF HOMES, SHADE TREES ON SOUTH SIDE.

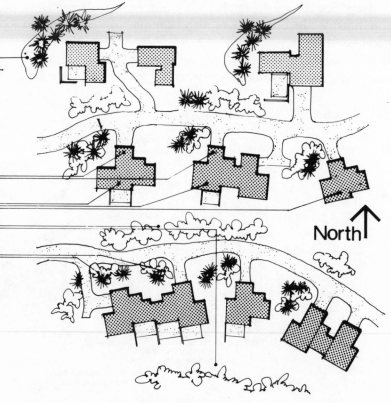

Passive solar can work in entire communities of single-family or multifamily units by orienting streets running east and west to maximize north and south exposures. SOURCE: John D. Bloodgood A.I.A.

natural insulating characteristics. Berming can be as simple as extending earth up around the foundation wall. On the south and west sides, landscaping with deciduous trees can provide shade to glazed areas during summer months to help keep the house cool. In winter, deciduous trees lose their leaves, allowing greater solar heat gain through glazed areas.

Orientation and landscaping alone can make a sizable difference in energy consumption and savings. In one study, an architect from New York state calculated that proper landscaping to shade the house in summer and buffer the house from cold winds in winter could produce overall energy savings up to about 15 percent.

While proper orientation is important in building a single passive solar house, extra attention must be paid in laying out an entire subdivision or community of passive solar houses or townhouses. Streets that run east and west will provide the maximum number of sites with north and south orientations, whether in a single-family or multifamily development. In single-family units, when possible, garages should be oriented to the north and living spaces to the south. Landscaping and privacy fencing can also be used to buffer the house from cold winter winds.

In multifamily developments, greenbelt areas can be used to landscape the units for maximum passive solar benefits in summer and winter. Again, garages should be placed on the north or northwest side of the buildings for energy efficiency.

Clustered or multifamily units, in general, provide one of the best opportunities for natural energy savings by reducing exposed exterior walls. By sharing one or two common walls, a unit naturally has less exposure, increasing the unit's energy efficiency. Major living spaces in multifamily units also should be oriented to the south whenever possible.

But just as the arrangement of glazed areas in single and multifamily units increases passive solar heat gain in winter, window placement can be used to increase natural ventilation in summer. Operable windows should be placed on adjacent sides of the house, whenever possible, to help promote air currents through the house. Openings on the south side of the house should be complemented with operable windows on the east or west side for the air to escape. This arrangement helps promote

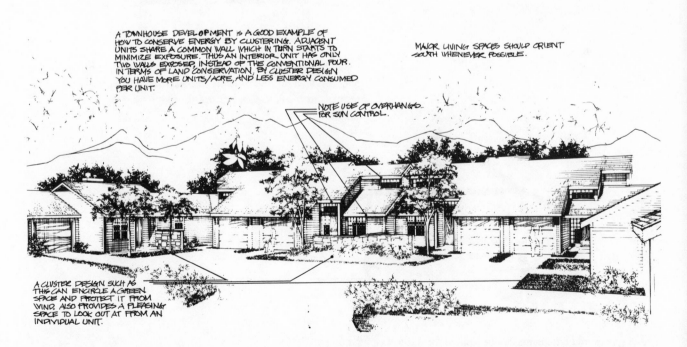

Multifamily developments and attached units such as townhomes are inherently more energy-efficient by reducing the amount of exposed walls in each unit. SOURCE: John D. Bloodgood A.I.A.

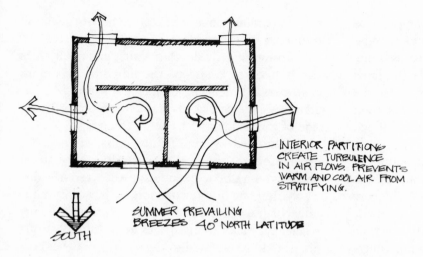

INTERIOR PARTITIONS
CREATE TURBULENCE
IN AIR FLOWS. PREVENTS
WARM AND COOL AIR FROM
STRATIFYING.

SUMMER PREVAILING
BREEZES 40° NORTH LATITUDE

SOUTH

Windows on adjacent sides of the house help create turbulence for increased ventilation potential.

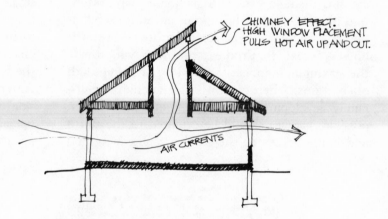

CHIMNEY EFFECT.
HIGH WINDOW PLACEMENT
PULLS HOT AIR UP AND OUT.

AIR CURRENTS

Operable clerestory windows create a chimney effect by exhausting hot, stratified air and drawing in cooler air, increasing air currents throughout the house for natural ventilation.

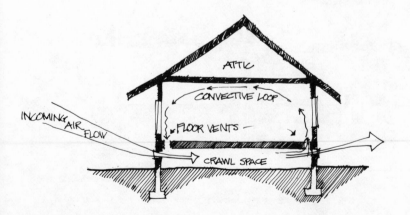

ATTIC

CONVECTIVE LOOP

FLOOR VENTS

INCOMING AIR FLOW

CRAWL SPACE

Crawl spaces and basements can be utilized for natural ventilation by creating a convective loop within living spaces. Floor vents control air movement. SOURCE: John D. Bloodgood A.I.A.

greater air turbulence and cooling benefits than just front-to-back channelized air movement.

In addition, operable windows in clerestories and stairwells produce a cooling "chimney effect." These windows can help cool the house by venting off warm air that has risen and accumulated in high ceiling areas. Air movement is increased by letting hot, stratified air escape and cool air be drawn in through low intake openings. Greenhouses or roof-glass spaces should include venting windows (or other means of ventilation such as an exhaust fan) to prevent heat build-up in these areas during summer months.

A chimney effect can be produced in sunspaces or greenhouses by providing both low intake openings and high exhaust openings. Also, use of sliding glass doors in sunspaces and south-facing living areas provides a dual benefit by maximizing solar heat gain in winter *and* natural cooling when opened in summer months.

In southern climates, cooler air in crawl spaces and basements can be used to promote natural convection currents through windows. Building the house on risers has the same effect. It should be noted that low, dense shrubbery near low windows can prevent maximum air flow through these openings. In addition, landscaping for shading in summer also should not be overdone. Too many shade trees can block needed sun in cool, early spring months.

Architectural elements can be used to provide needed shading. Roof overhangs play an important role in shading glazed areas in summer months.

Because the angle of the sun is lower in winter than in summer, an overhang can shade a glazed area in summer while letting the sun penetrate the living area or sunspace in winter. An operable awning can also produce the same shading opportunity.

The proper width for an overhang is calculated on the basis of latitude and the height of the glazed areas. A floor-to-ceiling window, for instance, requires a wider overhang to provide proper shading. A thirty-inch overhang, including gutter, located sixteen inches above a fifty-inch window (from sill to head) is appropriate for most locations between 30 and 50 degrees latitude, according to the Small Homes and Building Research Council of the University of Illinois in Champaign, Illinois.

Porches and trellis extensions also can serve as overhangs, particularly on east and west elevations to shade windows needed for ventilation. When designed carefully, overhangs, porches, wing walls, and trellises add exterior appeal in addition to serving a functional role as a passive solar design element.

In addition, careful arrangement of windows in living and work areas provides the energy saving benefits of natural lighting, decreasing the need for artificial functional lighting. Daylighting can help reduce electrical consumption in buildings considerably, in both residential and commercial applications, by taking advantage of light through windows and skylights.

Passive solar components, designs, construction and landscaping techniques, and architectural styles will vary slightly according to the goals ex-

Overhangs should be incorporated for solar control. Because the angle of the sun changes between summer and winter, an overhang can allow solar heat gain within the structure in the winter while shading glazed areas in summer.
SOURCE: Small Homes and Building Research Council, University of Illinois.

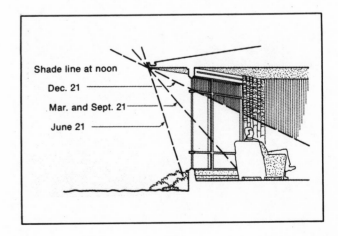

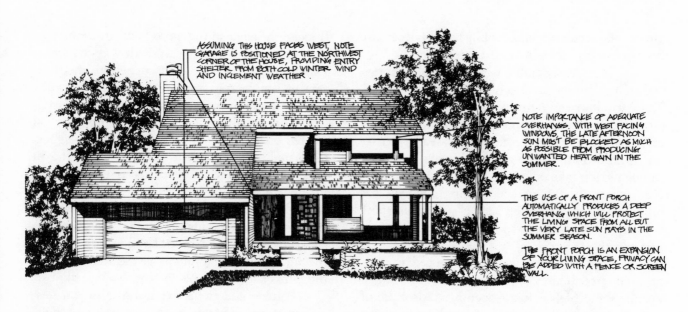

ASSUMING THIS HOUSE FACES WEST, NOTE GARAGE IS POSITIONED AT THE NORTHWEST CORNER OF THE HOUSE, PROVIDING ENTRY SHELTER FROM BOTH COLD WINTER WIND AND INCLEMENT WEATHER.

NOTE IMPORTANCE OF ADEQUATE OVERHANGS. WITH WEST FACING WINDOWS, THE LATE AFTERNOON SUN MUST BE BLOCKED AS MUCH AS POSSIBLE FROM PRODUCING UNWANTED HEAT GAIN IN THE SUMMER.

THE USE OF A FRONT PORCH AUTOMATICALLY PRODUCES A DEEP OVERHANG WHICH WILL PROTECT THE LIVING SPACE FROM ALL BUT THE VERY LATE SUN RAYS IN THE SUMMER SEASON.

THE FRONT PORCH IS AN EXPANSION OF YOUR LIVING SPACE. PRIVACY CAN BE ADDED WITH A FENCE OR SCREEN WALL.

Overhangs are important in controlling solar radiation in summer months by shading glazed areas. SOURCE: John D. Bloodgood A.I.A.

pected to be achieved in heating, cooling, daylighting, and satisfying buyer demand. House designs in different climatic regions, for instance, will vary to minimize overheating in southern climates and heat loss in northern areas.

The percentage of expected passive solar savings will vary from region to region as well, depending on a number of factors. Passive solar perfor-

mance is affected by climate, latitude, available solar radiation, topography, and surrounding vegetation. The building type, thermal requirements, amount of glazing, and occupant comfort level will also affect the performance of a passive solar home and will help determine the percentage of the home's dependence on conventional sources of heating and cooling.

Builders and architects have worked diligently to integrate solar principles in construction practices. Public and private research and development includes many demonstration projects such as this solar house sponsored under a program by Pennsylvania Power and Light.

2

RESEARCH AND DEVELOPMENT

The knowledge that the sun could be used to help heat buildings was not new to anyone, including builders. It was a fact of physical science and had been utilized throughout the history of regional architecture. But in the years following World War II, energy supplies were abundant and inexpensive. The sun was largely forgotten as an alternative source of heat. It became a forgotten art of construction. The energy crises of the early 1970s changed attitudes. Consumers demanded smaller, fuel-efficient cars and well-insulated and energy-efficient homes in the face of escalating energy costs. But even then, many builders were skeptical about the use of solar heat in the modern marketplace. Much of the technology and many of the mechanical systems were largely untested in actual homes.

Theory and history were fine for the textbooks and technology for the scientists. But builders needed to know: Can solar energy work on the construction site and in today's market? There was only one way to find out—experience. It was the builders' classroom. But builders were reluctant. Solar construction carried high financial risks. Builders needed funding to help reduce the high risks of trying something for the first time. Solar demonstration programs became the vehicle.

Beginning in the mid-1970s, demonstration programs for the construction of solar homes were conducted and sponsored by many groups including the Department of Housing and Urban Development, the Department of Energy (formerly known as the Energy Research and Development Administration), regional energy groups, home builders associations, universities, utility companies, and manufacturers of solar components. All of the demonstration programs had at least one purpose in common: helping the builder learn the techniques of solar construction.

As a result, many builders took a first or second look at solar energy as a primary or supplemental source of heat and water heating in homes. Solar homes cropped up across the country. The federal solar information center estimated that active solar installations increased from about 20,000 in 1974 to about 300,000 in 1981. The number of passive solar installations was comparatively small, due to a lack of federal incentives which had been initially awarded only to active solar systems. Passive solar systems, however, increased from several hundred in 1977 to an estimated 25,000 in 1981. In the course of its five-year residential solar demonstration program, HUD helped to fund the installation of solar space-heating and domestic water-heating systems in nearly 12,000 houses and apartment units.

While much information was derived from the construction experience in other demonstration programs, the HUD residential solar grant program was, perhaps, the largest single program geared most directly to helping home builders. It provided construction and operating experience. It provided performance data that were vital to evaluating systems and working out the bugs. But it also demonstrated how solar worked in the marketplace—the builder's vital relationship with the home buyer.

The $60 million HUD program was mandated by Congress as part of the Solar Heating and Cooling Demonstration Act of 1974. It was initiated in 1975 to demonstrate the widespread potential of solar energy for heating and cooling residential dwellings. Demonstration projects ranged from Maine to Hawaii, from custom homes to multifamily apartments. Both passive and active solar projects were included. Initially emphasis was placed on active solar systems, but by the end of the funding program, the focus had shifted to passive solar installations and to those incorporating both passive and active systems.

Builder attitudes about the solar grant program varied from one end of the spectrum to the other. The entire program was criticized on a number of accounts by the building industry as a whole and by participating individual builders. While most of the builders were grateful for the funding, many were discouraged at the resulting red tape. "Seeking the HUD grant was a mistake," said one California builder. "There was tremendous paperwork, and a payment on one part of the grant was two months overdue." A Utah builder also had problems. "The paperwork on this HUD project was extremely heavy and detailed." But despite heavy criticism, many lessons about solar construction were learned not only by those builders who participated, but by the entire building industry. Those lessons in practical solar construction made the program worthwhile.

In two separate surveys in the midst of the program in 1977 and 1979, *Professional Builder* magazine interviewed builders who participated in the five cycles of the solar demonstration program. Most of the builders indicated that they considered the demonstration program a good learning experience. "I wanted to get in on the ground floor," one builder from North Carolina remarked. Several builders mentioned that they had previously tried to experiment with solar on their own. But, they said, the HUD grant enabled them to gain experience on a larger scale. That was, perhaps, the most valuable result of the program: it enabled builders

Would You Have Installed a System Without a Grant?

Without the aid of the HUD residential solar demonstration program, most of the participating builders would not have installed a solar system, according to *Professional Builder's* 1979 survey of builders in the grant program. Expense was a major barrier. Without a grant some indicated that they would have tried solar on a small scale or only with passive features.

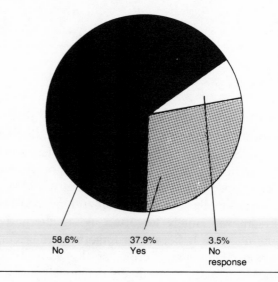

58.6%   37.9%   3.5%
No   Yes   No
                  response

across the country to learn what solar construction was all about.

That experience went far beyond the five-year program. While thousands of homes and apartments were constructed with the aid of the solar grants, the experience of the program encouraged many builders to continue pursuing solar. One Arizona builder said that the HUD grant helped launch him as a solar builder in his area. Consultants and advisors helped him get his start. "There were some very effective people in the HUD program to assist me," he said. And about one-third of the participating builders indicated in the *Professional Builder* survey that the HUD funding provided the necessary financial incentive to get started in solar. The grants were designed to help defray the high initial costs for solar equipment and installation, which were considered the greatest single barrier to the widespread commercialization of solar equipment.

The cost for the GLS Construction Co. of Winston-Salem, North Carolina, to install a solar system, for example, overran their grant of $7,000 per unit by about 50 percent on their first unit. According to its president Carl D. Lawson, they expected the grant to cover the cost of the system, but numerous problems and the newness of their venture added unforeseen costs to their first unit. Describing his experience as a "pioneering feeling," he added that he ran into "all problems that were humanly possible."

But Lawson was not discouraged. He felt that his next four solar units to be constructed in the HUD program would go much easier. His main problem with the first unit had been eliminated

---

Do You Now Offer Solar Heat or Hot Water in Your Homes?

Largely as a result of participating in the solar demonstration program, over half of the builders in *Professional Builder's* 1979 study said that they offered solar heating or hot water "on request," as a standard feature or as an option. Most of the builders who said that they do not offer solar in their homes typically encountered major problems in their grant homes.

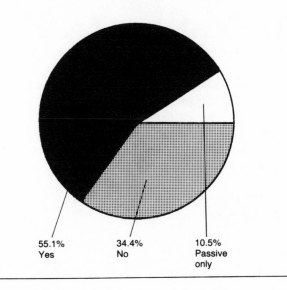

55.1%
Yes

34.4%
No

10.5%
Passive
only

---

through experience. With no trained technician to help, Lawson and his crews installed the system by the instruction manual and "common sense."

The high cost of solar was one of the most common complaints among builders. About one-half of the builders indicated that they would not have installed a solar system without a grant. But as a result of their experiences with solar, most builders changed their practices. Over one-half of the grantees indicated that they began offering solar heating or water heating in their other homes, most typically on custom homes or as an option in tract housing. Many builders also indicated that they provided active solar water-heating systems as standard features in their production housing. With the addition of those builders who include passive solar features only, over two-thirds of the respondents offered some type of solar system in their homes since their experience in the program. Many builders noted that they provided solar only on request.

Builder William G. Burdick of Birchwood, Wisconsin, had considered building solar without a HUD grant. The HUD solar grant program, however, gave him the encouragement and financial backing that he needed to get started. Due to his HUD experience, Burdick began offering solar as a standard in his home designs. But he considered the active solar panels only one part of his solar homes. In addition to the active solar flat-plate air collectors and rock storage, Burdick also included a greenhouse as a passive solar heat collector, a sunroom with large windows located above the rock storage area, and energy savers such as proper siting, window placement, and adequate insulation.

As in any new venture, many problems arose in construction and operation of the solar systems, but they were not bad enough to discourage most builders. For many, the experience was educational with long hours of homework, but they felt that they learned their lessons well.

The most common problems respondents to the *Professional Builder* survey encountered during construction included (in order): delays in the delivery of major components, lack of skilled installers, installation problems such as leaks and glass breakage, design shortcomings such as inade-

Did You Encounter Problems When Installing the System?

In a 1977 *Professional Builder* survey of builders participating in the HUD residential solar demonstration program, most indicated that they had problems installing or operating the solar systems, ranging from delivery delays to leaks and unskilled labor. But in a follow-up survey in 1979, other participating builders reported fewer problems and better delivery. Some builders faced minor adjustments in their systems, others encountered major problems; but optimism ran high among survey respondents.

	1977	1979
Installation problems (leaks)	20.0%	22.4%
Lack of skilled installers	22.6	18.9
Design shortcomings	13.3	17.2
Delays in delivery of components	32.0	15.5
System malfunctions	13.3	15.5
Other	13.3	—
None	26.6	34.4

(Adds to more than 100% due to multiple answers.)

quate heat storage space, and system malfunctions from pumps to valves.

But a surprising number of respondents to the survey said that they encountered no problems in construction or operation. One of these was architect William L. Burns of Burns & Peters Architects of Albuquerque, New Mexico. Using his experience in building other solar structures without grants, Burns designed a four-story, section-8 apartment complex for the elderly and handicapped using a concentrating collector for heat and hot water. Like builder Lawson, Burns used his experience to develop a successful solar system and to get to know the right components. Burns suggested that a contractor attempting to build solar homes or apartments for the first time should go step-by-step with a reliable manufacturer as an adviser.

Some of the barriers were real. Others were imagined. Some builders were concerned by the complexity of active solar technology. Almost half of the respondents to the *Professional Builder* survey said that they would like to see packaged solar systems by manufacturers that would ease installation. Many of these are still being developed in the early 1980s. "Manufacturers are selling their equipment, not a system," an Ohio builder remarked. Many builders also considered active solar equipment still to be in a "primitive" state. They requested better storage systems, more efficient collectors, warranties, and control over the industry in the form of system ratings.

In the late 1970s, builders still said that solar could not compete with conventional heating fuels, but many saw a decrease in payback periods as a result of soaring fuel costs. "It's getting better each year," a California builder said. "Solar is an excellent investment."

Other builders noted that while fuel costs have increased, so have the costs of solar equipment and installation, keeping payback about the same. Some builders felt that the term "payback" had been overused. For example, "a buyer doesn't think of payback in relation to air conditioning equipment," a Minnesota builder pointed out.

But still there was a dominating feeling among builders and buyers that solar was too expensive—particularly active solar systems. "As long as there is a reasonable monthly payment for other types of energy, people will not spend money for solar, not unless a lack of heating fuels will force them to do so," an Indiana builder said.

But even with some market resistance and reluctance among builders, many seemed to be glad that they participated in the demonstration pro-

Is Solar Energy Economically Feasible in Your Area?

In a 1979 study of builders who participated in the HUD solar demonstration program, almost half indicated that solar was too expensive to compete with conventional fuel systems. But they also noted that higher fuel prices may eventually prod buyers to consider solar as an economical investment.

Payback period too long	46.5%
Worthwhile investment	34.4
Solar hot water only	18.9
Passive solar systems only	10.3

(Adds to more than 100% due to multiple answers.)

gram. Many foresee a time when a non-solar house will be an obsolete product on the market, like gas-guzzlers in the automobile industry. Many of the participating builders agreed with one Colorado builder's statement: "When it's economical, we're prepared."

The HUD residential solar demonstration program, however, was undoubtedly and repeatedly criticized on many counts. Many questioned its effectiveness in stimulating the development of solar energy as an alternative or supplemental source of heat or water heating in homes and apartments. Others attacked the preliminary results of the program. In 1979, the General Accounting Office published a report that was severely critical of HUD's solar demonstration program. The GAO, the investigative arm of Congress, found serious performance problems with more than half of the ninety-one residential units built under the program that it examined. "We believe these problems can seriously impair not only the success of the program, but also the future of solar energy, since they indicate to the public that solar heating systems easily break down or perform poorly," the report said.

GAO and HUD locked horns over the report. And GAO seemed to miss the point that the demonstration program was designed not only to demonstrate the viability of solar energy to the public, but perhaps more importantly, to provide builders with practical experience in constructing solar homes and working out the problems.

In the report, GAO recommended that HUD use a $3 million contingency fund to help builders participating in the demonstration program repair problem systems. HUD said that a formal contingency fund had never been established. HUD, however, provided valuable consulting assistance to builders who had construction problems or difficulties in operating the solar systems. Some assistance was also provided by equipment manufacturers.

The report, entitled "Federal Demonstrations of Solar Heating and Cooling of Private Residences—Only Limited Success," also charged that the HUD program had failed to demonstrate the economic viability of solar heating systems. HUD countered that charge by pointing out that the GAO's economic analysis was based on only 5 of the 4,824 units that had been completed at the time. GAO had found one project with a payback period of eight to ten years, but the other four units studied were not expected to pay for themselves in fewer than seventeen years.

Some of the criticisms of the HUD program were based on solid ground. There were many problems. But it also should be pointed out that there were many successes as well. As for the builders involved in the demonstration projects, HUD reported three most commonly mentioned complaints: lack of information from manufacturers, inadequate quality control, and a shortage of skilled installers. It was encouraging, however, that the initial problems that were reported decreased as in-the-field experience increased. For example, 95 percent of the first group of builders to receive HUD grants reported that the systems overheated during the summer. In the second group, only 12 percent reported problems with overheating.

One important part of the demonstration program was the dissemination of information on the projects, not only the successful installations, but also solutions to construction and performance problems. Sources of data from HUD were basically derived from three different sources. First, about 15 percent of the grant houses were instrumented through the National Solar Data Network to collect data on the performance of the systems. Systems with poor performance typically reported significant design or installation problems. The most frequently mentioned performance problem was the loss of collected solar heat through transport, storage, or control malfunctions.

Second, utility bills on the solar grant houses and on non-solar houses were compared. Houses in the same locales were compared. Similar house style, size, and market characteristics were taken into consideration for comparison purposes. In a performance report released by HUD, over two-thirds of the solar houses used less total gas or electric energy than comparable houses in the same locality. Solar projects with gas backup heating systems used an average of 49 percent of the consumption of the houses without solar. Solar houses with electric backup heating systems used about 63 percent of the energy consumed by non-solar houses.

Other performance results were obtained through reports from field representatives concerning problems that occurred during the design, construction, or operational stages of the projects.

The purposes in studying the projects were many. On a builder's scale, the results help identify certain problems that can adversely affect the performance of residential space-heating and domestic water-heating systems.

Of about one hundred and ten solar-heated sites that were monitored in the National Solar Data Network, about 48 percent were built under HUD as residential demonstrations and 52 percent under DOE as commercial sites. Data gathered on these sites were used not only to report the performance of the various systems individually and collectively, but also to compare efficiencies of different types of systems and installations. Data were also used to identify and correct problems in the individual installations.

The information was collected by computer sensors for the amount of insolation on the collector array, ambient temperature, system flow rate and temperature, storage inlet and outlet temperature and flow rate, storage temperature, and auxiliary fuel-flow rates. Information was recorded by a microprocessor every five minutes and transmitted to the Automation Industries Inc. of Silver Spring, Maryland, a division of Vitro Laboratories. The information was evaluated and analyzed by a central computer. Monthly performance reports were issued.

Collected data helped to reveal a summary of problems encountered in the various demonstration projects. About 32 percent of the problems involved the collectors, including poor performance, leakage, poor maintenance, corrosion, and freezing. About 10 percent of the problems concerned storage, including pump failure, tank repairs for leakage and insulation, freezing, and corrosion. Heating subsystems accounted for about 27 percent of the reported problems including undersized design, air system leakages such as dampers, and failure of the air handling unit blower. Faulty controls caused about 18 percent of the problems ranging from improper cycling settings and on-site tampering to electrical and mechanical failures. The data derived from the monitoring program emphasized

that simplicity of design reduces the possibility and occurrence of operating problems.

In a 1978 report on the performance of solar systems installed under the HUD demonstration program, William Freeborne, a HUD solar engineer, concluded that many of the problems encountered in the solar installations could have easily been avoided. "It would seem that many of the problems which have taken months to correct could have been detected by a careful checkout before the contractors leave the job site," he said. "Many of the subsystem problems have taken months of instrumentation surveillance to correct. In the future, these problems will be taken care of during the checkout phase."

Unless builders pay attention to lessons learned in the HUD demonstration program, they will stumble into the same pitfalls, said Fred Morse, director of the DOE Office of Solar Applications. Some of the mistakes reported in the program included: uninsulated pipes, shading of collector areas, corrosion caused by the juxtaposition of incompatible materials, overly complex controls, improper equipment sizing, poor installation, and other simple mistakes. As builders and manufacturers gained experience, the occurrence of problems decreased greatly. Performance data on active solar systems, it was reported, were substantially degraded by uncontrolled heat losses from storage and transport of collected solar heat.

HUD concluded that the three key factors affecting the performance of solar systems were the quality of equipment, soundness of design, and, most important, competence of installation. HUD recommended that installation quality should meet or exceed current good HVAC practice.

The actual solar contribution for many of the active solar space-heating systems was below the predictions for most of the projects. Active space heating systems that were monitored contributed about half as much energy as predicted. Solar contributions on these projects ranged from about 4 to 45 percent. Domestic water heating systems averaged about 38 percent solar contribution, less than the predicted 53 percent. But it was also reported that many of the active solar systems performed better than had been predicted, saving even more conventional fuel than expected. HUD believed that the results from the demonstration program could improve performance of subsequent solar houses based on the lessons learned in the earlier projects.

While the early cycles of the program were devoted largely to the installation of active solar systems, the fifth and final round of grants was awarded to passive solar designs or systems which incorporated both active solar equipment and passive solar techniques. And the passive solar systems turned out to be the stars of the grant program. In one hundred monitored passive solar homes, an average of 80 percent of the heating loads were produced by the sun, according to J. Douglas Balcomb of the Los Alamos Scientific Laboratory, a recognized leader in the field of passive solar energy. In the monitored passive solar homes, temperature swings commonly ran an acceptable 5 to 10 Fahrenheit degrees. Wide-ranging interior temperature swings were often a major problem in passive solar systems in the past.

The passive solar systems were also generally the least expensive to construct. Cost studies showed that passive solar systems averaged about $7.70 per square foot of glazed area during the demonstration program; active solar domestic water heating systems averaged about $41 per square foot; active solar space heating averaged $48 per square foot; and active solar space cooling averaged $94 per square foot. Studies also pointed out that passive solar systems entailed virtually no maintenance or operating expense compared with active solar systems.

The HUD grant program served as the single largest training ground for solar construction. It brought design principles and theoretical data to the builders' level by letting builders learn for themselves. As expected, there were successes and failures. But the program served its purpose. It gave valuable solar experience to builders while attracting the attention of the marketplace to practical solar applications. It produced the initial surge of interest in solar energy among the building industry and the public. And as a result, many additional publicly and privately funded demonstration programs were born to continue the research and demonstration.

It was a good beginning. It set the stage.

Tour of Solar Homes Encouraged Builders to "Go Solar"

The federally sponsored residential solar demonstration program by the Department of Housing and Urban Development successfully provided participating builders solar experience. It was also successful on another front. It encouraged other public and private groups to produce their own solar demonstration programs. Home builder associations proved to be a good base from which to initiate interest among builders.

As a result of these scattered demonstrations—some featuring only one house, others with several models—builders gained valuable construction and design experience. They also learned that while a solar house can attract crowds of curiosity seekers, it can draw prospective home buyers as well.

A three-week open house tour of twelve solar homes in the metropolitan Denver area in early 1981 resulted in ninety thousand visitors to the homes, twenty-six immediate additional contracts for solar homes, and valuable solar construction experience for the participating builders.

About fourteen builders participated in the local program, although only twelve of the homes were ready for the tour in February and March 1981. The houses were scattered in twelve different locations throughout the metro-Denver area. Designed to promote the marketability of solar among the public and participating builders, the pilot program was developed by the Home Builders Association of Metro Denver in cooperation with the Department of Energy, the Solar Energy Research Institute, the Colorado branch of the Western Solar Utilization Network, and the Colorado Office of Energy Conservation.

Most of the visitors, the builders found, came with inquiring minds. But as the sales figures showed, some even came with money. And within six months of the tour, the twelve participating builders estimated a total of about $6.3 million in additional sales of solar homes. One builder conducted site plan changes to accommodate solar in his entire subdivision. Another merchant builder developed a passive solar plan that can flop north/south, east/west depending on the lot.

In addition to exposing the public to attractive and affordable solar homes, the program was designed to provide established builders with a foot-in-the-door entry into building solar homes. One builder described his experience through the pilot program as "priceless."

More than three hundred local builders attended an introductory seminar which explained passive solar design principles as well as the purpose of the program. About forty-seven proposals were submitted for inclusion in the program, of which thirteen were selected. One builder, funded under another design program, was eventually included as part of the tour.

The Solar Energy Research Institute in Golden, Colorado, reimbursed design consultants for the passive solar designs. Builders had a simple, no-cost agreement with SERI to construct the houses. The houses were constructed by the builders under their own individual financing arrangements and were expected to be sold as any normal spec house. In addition to funding the design of the homes, SERI reimbursed the builders for the installation, operation, and maintenance of the monitoring equipment and for allowing the public tours.

By the end of the three-week tour, five of the demonstration houses had been sold, ranging in price from $56,500 to $142,000. Among those not sold by the end of the tour, one builder had three good prospective buyers and one of the houses was sold during an auction to raise funds for a local public television station.

As a result of the program, many of the participating builders developed and adapted plans to include solar. By the end of the tour, twenty-six additional contracts on solar homes had been taken by the builders and one builder reported thirty-nine reservations waiting to be signed. The pilot program was adapted for duplication in Portland, Oregon, in the fall of 1981.

The program participants included builders of merchant housing and semi-custom and custom homes.

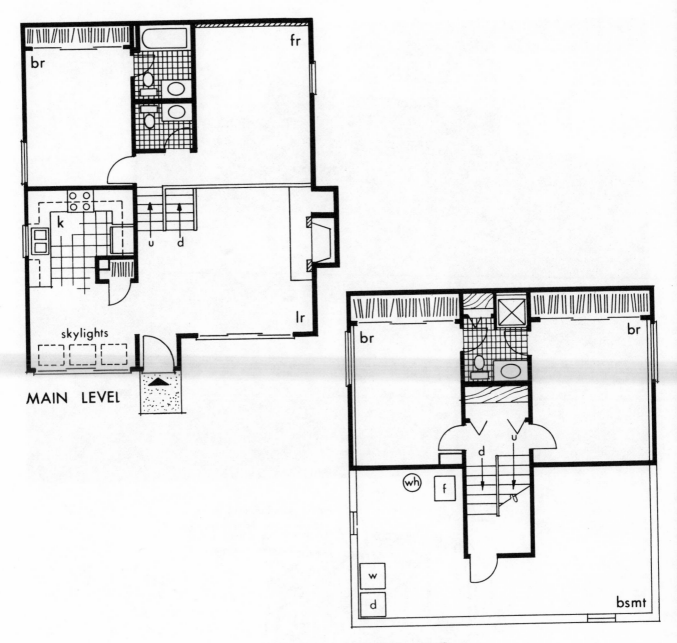

MAIN LEVEL

LOWER LEVEL

Alpert Corporation of Denver constructed a 1380-square-foot, tri-level in Aurora, Colorado, for the tour. The house was an adaption of one of the firm's standard cluster home designs. The floorplan was adjusted and redesigned to provide better orientation to the sun. Based on a direct gain system, the house featured increased use of glass on the south-facing exposure, reduced use of windows on the east and west exposures, and no north-facing glass.

Other energy-saving features in the passive solar home included R30 ceiling insulation, R17 wall insulation, and a ceiling fan for increased air circulation throughout the house, aided by an open cathedral ceiling.

Designers Downing/Leach Associates estimated about 40 percent energy savings through the passive solar design and internal mass in the masonry floors and walls. Designed to be moderately priced, the three-bedroom/three-bath house sold during the tour for $78,500.

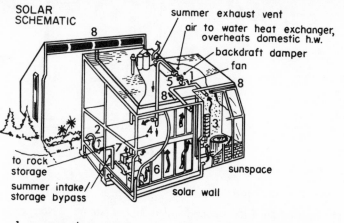

SOLAR
SCHEMATIC

summer exhaust vent
air to water heat exchanger,
overheats domestic h.w.
backdraft damper
fan

to rock
storage

summer intake/
storage bypass

solar wall

sunspace

1 sunspace/solar wall
parallel circuit to rock
storage in floor slab

2 passive radiant heat
distribution from slab

3 direct heat gain into
water tubes, floor, and
concrete aggregate wall

4 storage bypass to heat air

5 hot water preheater

6 h.w. collectors for hot tub

7 fireplace air heater

8 overhang / screen
sun control

Another house located in Greenwood Commons, a solar subdivision in Boulder, Colorado, included active and passive solar features.

Active solar water heating was included to pre-heat water for domestic use and for the hot tub. Passive solar design techniques included a two-story sunspace that contained a 12-inch-thick aggregate concrete trombe wall and four 450-gallon fiberglass water tubes for thermal mass. A 300-cubic-foot thermal rock storage area was located under the concrete slab floor for storage of solar heat gain in the sunspace. The sunspace was located adjacent to living and dining areas as well as two bedrooms above.

Other energy savers included R22 wall insulation, R32 ceiling insulation, an airlock entry, berming on the north side of the house to help reduce heat loss, and a brick-enclosed two-face fireplace.

The 2200-square-foot, three-bedroom house was designed by architects Rudolf B. Lobato Associates of Longmont, Colorado. Heritage Construction of Boulder, Colorado was the builder. The split-level house was priced at $168,500.

A 1550-square-foot, passive solar bi-level plan by Tradition Homes Ltd. revolves around a south-facing solar atrium on the rear elevation. The atrium includes an 8-inch-thick thermal mass wall and concrete floors with quarry tile for storage of solar heat. A second-story balcony overlooks the atrium area. Other energy savers included 2 × 6 walls, airlock entry, R38 ceiling insulation, R19 wall insulation plus R5 insulated sheathing, and 2-inch foundation perimeter insulation. Ceiling fans aid heat circulation in winter and natural cooling in summer months. A 12/12 roof pitch was designed to accommodate active solar space heating and water heating in the future.

Priced from $87,900, the three-bedroom house was built by Tradition Homes of Boulder, Colorado, and designed by McCaffrey and Welch. As a result of the program, Tradition Homes completed a second passive solar design for their subdivision which could flip-flop north/south, east/west, depending on the lot. They also modified their original land plot arrangements to accommodate solar considerations.

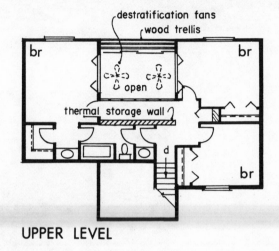

UPPER LEVEL

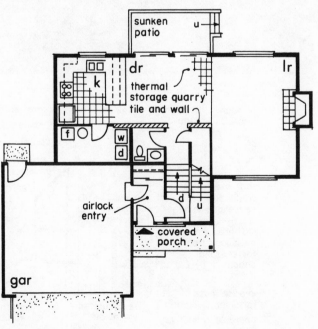

LOWER LEVEL

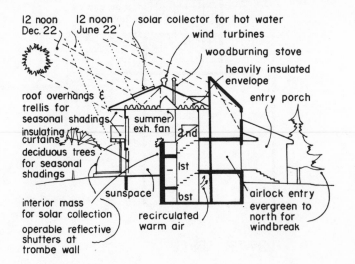

12 noon
Dec. 22

12 noon
June 22

solar collector for hot water

wind turbines

woodburning stove

heavily insulated
envelope

entry porch

roof overhangs &
trellis for
seasonal shadings

insulating
curtains

deciduous trees
for seasonal
shadings

summer
exh. fan

2nd

1st

bst

interior mass
for solar collection

sunspace

operable reflective
shutters at
trombe wall

recirculated
warm air

airlock entry

evergreen to
north for
windbreak

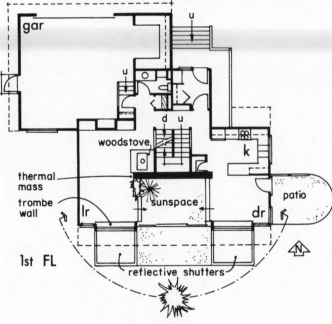

The 1900-square-foot, three-bedroom house designed to integrate solar into interior space design, included both an active solar water-heating system and passive solar design techniques.

Features included a centralized sunspace with trombe walls, active solar water heating, a centralized wood-burning stove, insulated shutters, R8-insulated foundation, R30 ceiling insulation, R19 wall insulation, and an airlock entry.

Major living spaces were designed around the central sunspace to maximize natural heat and light. Trombe walls in the sunspace helped to retain solar heat gain. Reflective

exterior shutters were designed to cover the trombe walls to minimize heat loss on winter nights and overheating in summer.

Placement of the garage provided a thermal buffer and windbreak for the main part of the house. A south-sloping roof was designed to accommodate photovoltaic solar cells in the future, when they are deemed economically feasible for residential use.

Built by Kurowski Development Co. of Littleton, Colorado, the two-story house was priced about $139,900 and located in The Ranch, a high-end, planned community. It was designed by David Barrett of Sunflower Architects.

Ferguson Construction Co. of Lakewood, Colorado, built a five-bedroom, 3200-square-foot house, incorporating direct gain and thermal-mass passive solar techniques as well as active solar water heating.

The passive solar design was designed to provide about 50 percent of the home's heating needs. The sun's rays flow through a south-facing window wall. The solar heat is absorbed by cylinders of water, masonry, and a quarry-tile floor. A curving brick trombe wall was also included for solar heat storage. A fan and ducting system aid in circulating heat in winter and natural cooling in summer.

The active solar water heating system was designed to supply 85 percent of hot water needs. Overall, the house was expected to save about 80 percent on heating costs for the home. Other energy-saving features included a greenhouse, R20 wall insulation, R30 ceiling insulation, two woodburning stoves, an electronic ignition furnace, and an airlock vestibule with a clerestory design.

Designed by Atkinson-Karius Architects, the house was priced at $199,000.

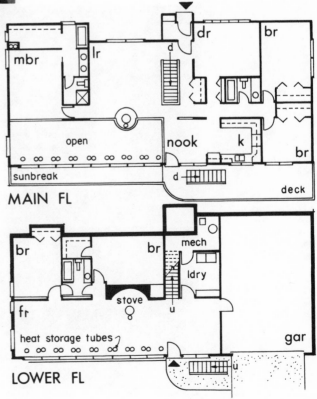

MAIN FL

LOWER FL

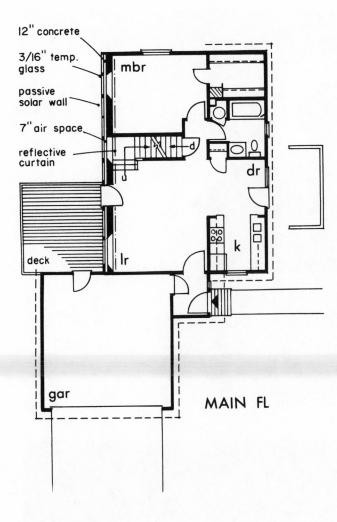

12" concrete

3/16" temp. glass

passive solar wall

7" air space

reflective curtain

mbr

dr

d

deck

lr

k

gar

MAIN FL

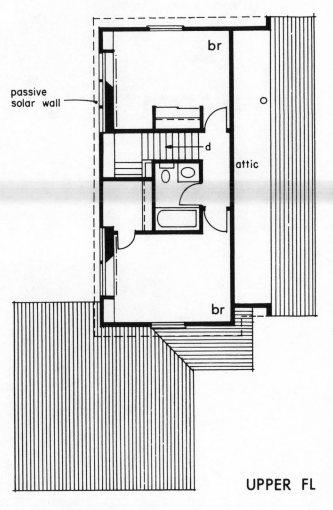

passive solar wall

br

d

attic

br

UPPER FL

For the solar tour, U. S. Homes' Witkin Southeast division constructed a 1232-square-foot, three-bedroom, two-story house in Aurora, Colorado.

Features in the passive solar SunUser house included R30 ceiling insulation, R19 wall insulation, 2 × 6 exterior wall framing, reduced window exposure to the north, double entry, reflective curtains, and a trombe wall which was designed to provide about 55 percent of the home's heating needs. The south-facing trombe wall consisted of a one-foot thick concrete mass wall glazed on the exterior with a 7-inch air space between the wall and glass. A vent at the top of the trombe wall air space was designed to help avoid overheating on warm days.

The house was sold in April 1981 during an auction to benefit the local public television station. Designed for affordability, the house was auctioned off at $72,500. It was designed by architect Dennis Holloway and solar consultant John Giltner.

A 1950-square-foot, three-bedroom ranch in the Denver tour featured an attached greenhouse, airlock entry, R19 wall insulation, R30 ceiling insulation, and active solar water heating.

Extensive use of brick interior walls for thermal storage was estimated to contribute nearly 60 percent of the home's heating requirements. The great room, kitchen, and nook included brick paved flooring for passive solar heat retention.

The house was built by Unique Homes of Arvada, Colorado, and was designed by Michael Albanes and Michael Bush. It sold before the end of the tour for $142,000. Five other homes were also pre-sold during the tour.

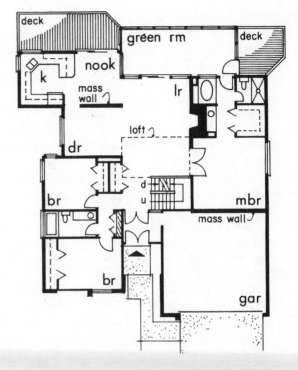

The 2295-square-foot, ranch-style home was designed to prove that passive and active solar provide a good combination for energy savings. It was constructed in Boulder, Colorado by The Arnold Group and designed by architects Richardson Nagy Martin with consultation by the Crowther Solar Group. It was priced about $150,000.

As a result of the Denver tour of solar homes, The Arnold Group planned to "solarize" an entire 134 single-family home community. Site plans were changed to provide needed solar access for the homes.

Water heating for the tour home was supplied by an active solar system. Passive solar ideas included a direct-gain solar room with a vaulted ceiling, tile floors, and brick wall as a storage medium for solar heat. Thermostatically controlled fans redistribute stratified hot air from the top of the sunspace and distribute the heat through ducting into the basement for storage.

A clerestory window and exposed brick wall were included in the living room for direct heat gain and retention. The northern exposure of the house was windowless to reduce heat loss. Glazed areas were used, instead, extensively on the southern exposure.

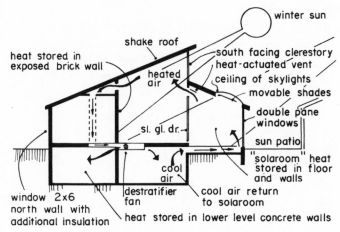

Model Home Demonstrates Solar Concepts for the Future

Home builder associations have sponsored several solar home demonstrations throughout the country. But the research home shown here was sponsored by a different sort of association—the Copper Development Association of Stamford, Connecticut.

Called the Suntronic house and located in Greenwich, Connecticut, the house was designed not to reflect immediate trends, but to demonstrate concepts which would be developed in the coming years. The 5200-square-foot Suntronic house was constructed in 1980 and included products from twenty industry participants.

Designed by Berkus Group Architects, the house incorporated the latest and most innovative ideas in energy efficiency, solar energy, and housing design.

Many areas in the house fulfilled a dual purpose, combining living space with function. The two-story, double-glazed greenhouse, for example, was a good solution for including a hot tub in inclement areas. "It provides a controlled environment that can be used year-round in northern climates," Berkus said. In addition to serving as an activity area adjacent to the lower level family room, it added natural light and interior landscaping to the overlooking living room.

But the greenhouse also was a passive solar design element. Solar heat gain is absorbed by the thermal-mass floor and an experimental copper-tube water-storage wall for heat storage and distribution throughout the house as needed. The greenhouse walls consisted of thick masonry block. The floor was covered with slate. The thermal mass aids in minimizing temperature swings.

A column in the living room served as both a sculptural and structural element. The column also

A greenhouse facing south provided additional living space and the advantages of passive solar heat. Access to the greenhouse was provided through the lower level family room (shown). Note the water heat storage wall which was designed to absorb direct heat gain. An additional water wall was located in the master bedroom. PHOTO: Robert Perron.

The Suntronics house, sponsored by the Copper Development Association, was designed with energy management in mind. The front elevation of the house (shown) was buried on three sides by an earth berm to protect the house from cold winter winds. The rear elevation faced south for maximum direct heat gain from the sun.

Sculptural forms were used throughout the house to add aesthetic appeal. Large south-facing areas, an atrium entry, a greenhouse, and active solar collectors were used for energy efficiency. All three levels of the house are shown. PHOTOS: Robert Perron.

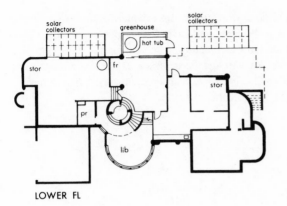

LOWER FL

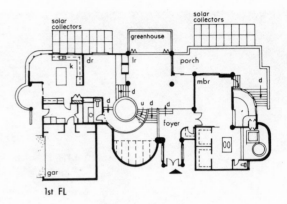

1st FL

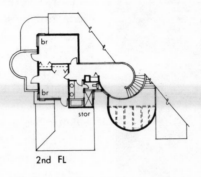

2nd FL

served as a duct for recycling heat from the high ceilings down to living spaces.

In addition to displaying new ideas in housing design, the idea house also was used to demonstrate and monitor heat loss, heat gain, and transmission. The house was oriented with major window areas on the southern exposure. Exposed exterior walls were minimized to reduce heat loss. The north, east, and west walls were largely buried into an earth berm.

The energy system incorporated design elements as well as mechanical equipment. Components included: large semi-circular skylights with thermal blankets to minimize heat loss in the master bath and library (see photo on next page); a double-glazed, two-story greenhouse with a hot tub and thermal mass floor; heat recycling columns in living areas; water storage walls for passive solar heat gain and retention, located in the walls of the

master bedroom and lower-level family room (see plans); 640 square feet of liquid, flat-plate active solar collectors for heat and water heating with storage in a 1000-gallon hot water tank in the basement; and a remote array of photovoltaic cells that convert sunlight directly into electricity.

The photovoltaic system provided electricity for the operation of the active solar system pumps and fans. Battery storage was designed to supply lighting for the house in case of emergency. A separate room in the basement contained 12-volt lead acid batteries for photovoltaic electricity storage. Zoned air-to-air heat pumps provided space cooling and auxiliary space heating. Cool, night-time air was also used to cool the house's thermal storage mass.

The library was designed as a control center. It contained a sophisticated home computer system with capacity for energy management of the house.

The library, located on an expanded stairway landing between the main and lower levels, included a master home management computer system to control energy efficiency. Heat loss through the skylight was reduced through use of a thermal blanket which covered the glazed area at night.
PHOTO: Robert Perron.

common as technology is applied to home management," Berkus noted. The computer center also controlled security and contained convenience programs such as household finance and schedules.

The energy systems were incorporated largely for experimentation and demonstration. But the design of the house was not subordinate to the mechanical system, Berkus said. Active solar collectors were separated from the architecture to allow for the advancement of technology and flexibility of design. As more efficient collectors and solar systems are developed, the mechanical equipment can be changed without altering the architectural design of the house.

"There are inevitable changes ahead in solar technology, so by putting the collectors on a platform, you have easier access. You can retrofit without touching the roof," Berkus explained. By separating the equipment from the architecture, a better opportunity for architectural expression, unhampered by restrictions imposed by mechanical equipment, was provided.

Other elements of the house also were designed for aesthetic appeal while maximizing energy efficiency. An air-lock entry vestibule reduces air infiltration, but glassed on both sides, it becomes an attractive atrium space.

The calculated contribution of active and passive solar energy to the space heating and domestic water heating was estimated at about 48 percent. The greenhouse was expected to provide about 10 percent of that contribution. The calculations, though, did not include direct gain through south-facing windows or the thermal contribution from the heat pipe walls.

The computer was programmed to help control utility costs in the home, ranging from maximizing equipment efficiency to anticipating changing weather conditions.

In response to temperature and humidity sensors throughout the house, the computer automatically controlled separate heating and cooling zones. Also, in monitoring the energy performance of the house, the computer measured and recorded temperature, solar radiation, barometric pressure, precipitation, wind speed and direction, internal and external relative humidity, and electric power consumption for each component. Periodic printed reports on the system performance, weather data, and energy consumption were issued by the computer.

"The computer center, incorporated in the library of the house, will become more and more

*Utility-Sponsored Passive Solar
Demonstration: Searching for Alternative
Heating Sources in Production Housing*

Utility companies have also participated in solar home demonstrations. The companies began to realize the importance of energy conservation and alternative sources of energy with the onset of energy shortages in the early 1970s. Solar energy, they realized, was one alternative to help conserve energy in homes, thereby reducing expensive peak loads and the need for new power stations to be constructed. And that could help keep energy costs lower.

Pennsylvania Power & Light initiated a passive solar demonstration program in 1981 for the construction of six cost-effective passive solar houses spread throughout its service area. The purpose of the program was "to find out the best integration of passive solar components to heat homes efficiently," said PP&L's Pete Roberts, manager of research and technical services. Passive solar was selected for the program because "it is simple, has no moving parts, and is easy to maintain," Roberts said.

The utility company had been investigating alternative forms of energy and conservation since 1973. Their energy conservation program began with a research home constructed in 1974. The thermal design principles were then incorporated into five other demonstration homes in 1976. Planning for the passive solar demonstration program began as early as 1978 with a study commissioned by PP&L on the practicability of passive solar space heating conducted by the Institute for Energy Conversion in Newark, Delaware. The study concluded that to have any significant impact on electrical energy loads passive solar homes would have to be median priced and able to be produced by tract builders. Construction techniques familiar to the average builder would have to be used for mass market construction. These homes also would have to reflect local preferences in architectural style and provide a noticeable cost benefit to the homeowners.

The six passive solar homes were completed in early 1981. PP&L selected six builders for construction of the homes, using the builders' standard designs, which were adapted to accommodate passive solar features. Two of the houses were completely redesigned, but still fit into the builders' standard line of homes.

Performance of the homes was expected to be monitored for thirty months. Each of the homes included a different combination of passive solar design techniques and components, including some ideas which were being field-tested for the first time and not available commercially at that time.

"We wanted to foster the introduction of passive solar techniques and technology into home construction," Roberts said. "We realized that to promote widespread use of passive solar, there had to be an emphasis on mass market designs. As a result of the program, many of the builders are now offering passive solar plans on their own."

In the demonstration program, PP&L provided funding for:

- Redesign of the builders' standard home plans to accommodate passive solar features by Doug Kelbaugh of Kelbaugh & Lee Architects in Princeton, New Jersey, and Don Prowler of South Street Design in Philadelphia;
- Technical assistance through engineering consultants;
- Incremental cost of the passive solar features, including any deviations from normal practice such as duct changes, which were over and above the cost of constructing the same house conventionally;
- Carrying costs during the sixty-day open houses;
- Equipment and operation of the monitoring.

In promoting the passive solar houses, each was open for a two-month period, staggered between February 26 and June 21, 1981. In total, 35,594 visitors toured the homes. After the open houses, the builders continued to keep the homes open as models. Monitoring of the houses began in the fall of 1981 after occupancy. The houses were designed to sell between $75,000 and $90,000. They ranged in size from 1584 to 2116 square feet.

Research data on the homes was expected to help PP&L develop recommendations on what builders and buyers could expect for the initial costs and subsequent energy-saving benefits of a passive

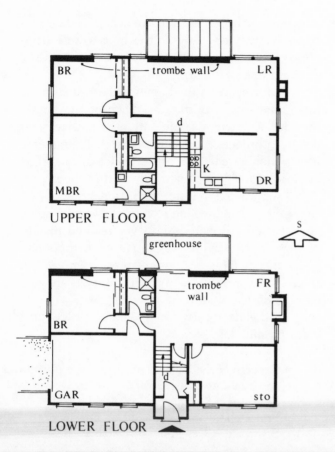

BR   ⟵ trombe wall ⟶   LR

d

MBR   K   DR

UPPER FLOOR

S

greenhouse

trombe wall   FR

BR

d

GAR   sto

LOWER FLOOR

The 2116-square-foot house was a learning experience for builder Arthur Axelrod of Axelrod Construction in Merion Station, Pennsylvania. It was his first passive solar house.

An attached greenhouse included a trombe wall for heat storage. Other passive solar features included thermosyphon preheating of domestic water and an eutectic salt assisted heat pump for supplemental heating and cooling. The house faced north. The house sold for $92,500 shortly after the open house.

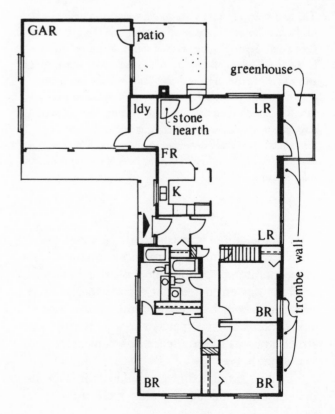

A standard, 1575-square-foot ranch model was modified with passive solar features including a non-vented trombe wall in two of the south-facing bedrooms, a mass wall in the greenhouse, glazed areas and a quarry-tile floor in the dining room, window quilts, and double-door entry vestibule, an attic vent fan for summer cooling, and 2 × 6 framing.

Built by Lundy Homes of Williamsport, Pennsylvania, the house also included radiant panels for backup auxiliary heating. It was listed for sale at $103,000, about 8 percent more than the comparable conventional model.

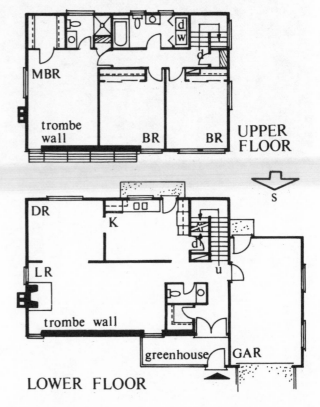

UPPER FLOOR

S

LOWER FLOOR

The two-story, 1650-square-foot house was a new design for builder Robert Sherman of Sherman & Walton Inc. in Lancaster, Pennsylvania. Facing south, a sunspace serves as a passive solar collector as well as a double-door vestibule entry to the house. The one-foot-thick trombe wall was core-filled concrete blocks covered with a selective foil surface for heat absorbancy. Auxiliary heating was supplied through an eutectic-salt-assisted heat pump. Water was heated conventionally during off-peak hours. The house was sold for $87,000, not including the cost of the experimental solar features.

solar home. Life-cycle costs will be developed by analyzing the actual construction costs and computer-monitored performance of the homes. In 1981, it was estimated that a passive solar home, providing about half of the home's heating needs, would cost about 10 percent more than the construction cost of living space in a comparable conventional house.

Those estimated costs would not include special experimental devices that were used in the

demonstration homes, but only those commercially available such as increased glazing, thermal storage mass in tile floors and trombe walls, and attached greenhouses or sunspaces.

The passive solar features in the homes were varied to compare performance of the different systems. The houses were located in six different regions of the service area to provide a wide variation in climate in the state. All of the houses included R42 ceilings, R24 walls, R10 foundation perimeter

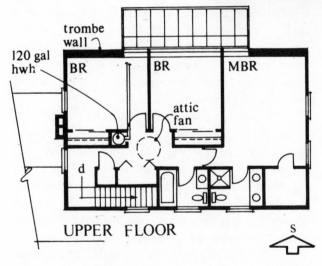

trombe wall

120 gal hwh

BR   BR   MBR

attic fan

d

UPPER FLOOR

S

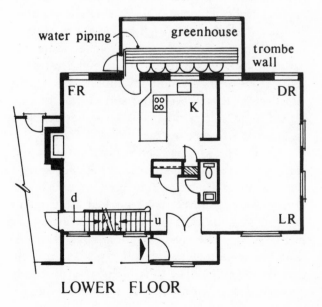

water piping   greenhouse   trombe wall

FR   K   DR

d

u

LR

LOWER FLOOR

The 1700-square-foot, two-story was a new design for builder Frank Pedriani of Pedriani Custom Built Homes in Mahonoy City, Pennsylvania. It was listed at $75,000. The north-facing house included trombe walls treated with a selective foil for better absorption of the sun's rays. Water was preheated through a thermosyphon system located in the greenhouse. Resistance baseboard provides backup heat and a whole-house ventilation fan helps keep the house cool in summer.

55

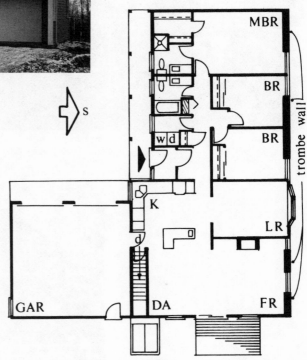

Located near Scranton in PP&L's northern region, the $79,900 ranch stirred up buyer interest in passive solar homes for builder Francis Cunion of Heritage Homes Ltd. in Olyphant, Pennsylvania.

Facing north, glazed areas were maximized on the southern exposure. Bedrooms and living areas were arranged to take advantage of the sun's natural heat. Service areas, the garage, bathrooms, and a double-door vestibule entry help buffer the north side of the house. Trombe walls were treated with the selective foil for maximum heat absorbancy. Water is heated conventionally during off-peak hours and supplemental heat is supplied through electric resistance baseboard heat.

The 1612-square-foot house was offered as a standard model, with a few modifications, for $67,500 in 1981 without land or improvements.

insulation, and R11-to-R19 floors over basement areas. All windows not facing south were triple glazed. Each of the houses also included an air-lock entry to reduce heat loss.

Five of the houses incorporated a trombe wall for thermal-mass heat storage. To help increase efficiency, a thin black foil was applied to the trombe walls. The selective surface foil was applied like wallpaper with adhesive to the poured concrete or block walls. The material absorbs more radiation and loses less heat through re-radiation, Roberts said, when compared with trombe walls just painted black. Compared to a triple-glazed trombe wall or one with movable insulation, the double-glazed trombe wall with the surface foil was expected to provide a 15 percent better net heat gain and cost less to construct, Roberts claimed.

Prototype windows and experimental glazings and films were used in some of the homes as well. But the most exotic feature used in two of the homes was an eutectic-salt-assisted heat pump. Eutectic salts are a storage medium consisting of a phase-change chemical which absorbs the sun's heat. Solar heat melts the salt crystals during the day. As the material cools at night, returning to its crystalized state, stored heat is transmitted into the

home. In a passive solar house, the eutectic salts could help prevent overheating problems, increase storage capacity, and decrease heat loss, Roberts said. In addition, air is circulated over the salts to preheat the air to the evaporator coil of the heat pump to help increase efficiency. The prototype heat pumps were developed using commercially available components.

Water for domestic use was preheated passively through thermosyphon systems in three of the houses. In the other houses, water was preheated conventionally during off-peak hours.

None of the builders reported any construction problems due to familiar construction techniques and building materials, although they were geared to passive solar design.

The builders reported favorable responses to the passive solar homes as a result of the open houses. In the northern region, builder Francis Cunion of Heritage Homes Ltd. in Olyphant, Pennsylvania, said that in the eyes of his buyers, "We're the solar people now." He has taken deposits to build other passive solar houses in other locations. "There was a lot of exposure and credibility as a result of being associated with a major utility," he said. The house was offered as a standard model

greenhouse

trombe wall

slate hearth

FR

K

LDY

LR

BR

GAR

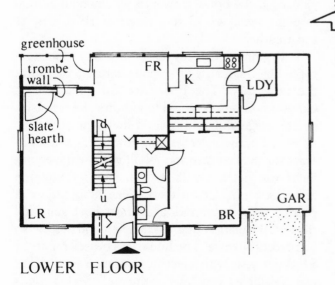

LOWER FLOOR

S

BR

skylight

BR

BR

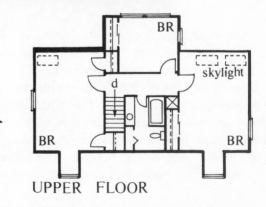

UPPER FLOOR

The 1823-square-foot Harrisburg model was modified from a standard plan of builder George Carlson of Dillsburg, Pennsylvania. The north-facing house included a 5 × 12 foot sunspace with a ventilation fan and a 12-inch thick trombe wall consisting of core-filled concrete block. Water was preheated by thermosyphon. Auxiliary heat was supplied by a conventional heat pump. Skylights were used for venting. Window quilts were used to help reduce heat loss through glazed areas. Low emittance glass was included in some windows. It was listed for sale at $85,900.

57

after the open house, selling in 1981 for $67,500 without land or improvements. Estimated energy savings were substantial. The passive solar house was estimated to cost about $185 to $250 per year to heat in 1981, compared with a cost in excess of $1000 to heat a comparable conventional home.

Builder George Carlson of Dillsburg, Pennsylvania (near Harrisburg), who also participated in the program, received many inquiries about passive solar new construction and remodeling. In addition to offering the demonstration plan in his standard model line, he began passive solar remodeling work as a result of his experience in the demonstration program.

Passive solar put a new light on his standard plan which was modified to accommodate passive solar. Living areas were opened up and window space was increased on the southern exposure, adding to the marketing appeal of the home. "We're cutting heating costs while building what people like in a home," Carlson said. "Passive solar is a marketable product."

An HBA, Utility, and University Team-up to Build an Experimental Solar House

A significant solar home experiment was also conducted by a team consisting of a builders' association, a utility company, and a university.

In cooperation with the Rochester Institute of Technology and the Rochester Gas and Electric Corporation, the Home Builders Association of Rochester, New York, helped build a prototype active and passive solar energy house on the university's campus. The house was completed in early 1978.

It was the first time that the home builders had participated in an experimental program, said the association's vice president Joseph F. McCue. He predicted that it probably would not be the last.

Although the house was constructed for the university for experimental purposes, "the association has never had as much participation in a project by its members," said McCue. "Over sixty builders and suppliers contributed materials and funds to the project." The association raised $30,000 among its members to help pay for labor

and materials. Hired by the association, Schantz Homes Inc. acted as the general contractor for the project.

The 1832-square-foot, three-bedroom house was designed specifically for energy savings, solar collection, and solar heat storage. For active solar space heating, 672 square feet of collectors were arranged on the rear elevation of the house which faced south. But the active solar system was only part of the energy savings.

Passive solar features included: heavy insulation with an R19-insulated foundation, R26-insulated walls, and R40-insulated ceilings; a bank of triple-glazed windows on the southern exposure; insulated steel doors; overhangs; a berm on the northern exposure to protect the house from cold winter winds; and an interior atrium for passive solar heat collection and aesthetic value. As a matter of fact, the house was so insulated, it had to be vented to reduce condensation. Some moisture problems occurred.

Basically the house was overbuilt and overdesigned for research purposes. Heat from the liquid flat-plate collectors was stored in four 1000-gallon tanks. The heating system also contained a solar-assisted heat pump, electric resistance heater, and an electric boiler which was only run in off-peak hours. Excluding land, the house cost about $100,000 in 1978, according to the university. The active solar system cost about 10 percent to 12 percent of the total cost.

Located in an area highly responsive to engineering, the house drew a crowd of about 10,000 in eight weekends in the winter of 1978, despite bad weather.

Beginning in May 1978, the house was occupied by the family of an engineering professor at the university. The Rochester Gas and Electric Corporation was expected to monitor the house for energy usage and savings for a four-year period.

The active solar system, however, did not operate for the first one-and-a-half years while equipment was being modified. But even without the active solar heat contribution, a combination of passive solar techniques and direct heat gain and the over-insulation resulted in a hefty 60 percent to 70 percent savings. The house was heated for about $300 per year with electric resistance heat. That was considered very low for the area, McCue said.

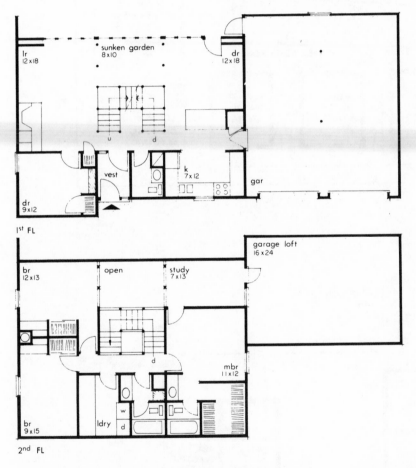

1ˢᵗ FL

2ⁿᵈ FL

The 1832-square-foot experimental energy house was located on the campus of the Rochester Institute of Technology in an area designated for faculty housing. The project was the brain-child of Dr. Richard A. Kenyon, Dr. Paul H. Wojciechowski, and architect John Fayko, and was constructed in cooperation with the Home Builders Association of Rochester, New York.

The floor plan was designed for better air circulation by eliminating some interior walls. The sunken garden atrium added aesthetic value as well as serving as a heat collector in winter. Note the mechanical core for the kitchen,

baths, laundry, and piping for the active solar collectors.

The active solar space heating system (shown on page 60) featured flat-plate, liquid-type collectors on the main roof. The drain-down system was designed for protection against freezing. The manufacturer was Sunworks.

The domestic solar water heating system (shown on page 60) featured tubular collectors located on the garage roof. The circulating fluid consisted of a 50 percent/50 percent mixture of water and propylene glycol. An antifreeze served as protection against freezing in this system. KTA was the manufacturer.

Active Solar Space-Heating System

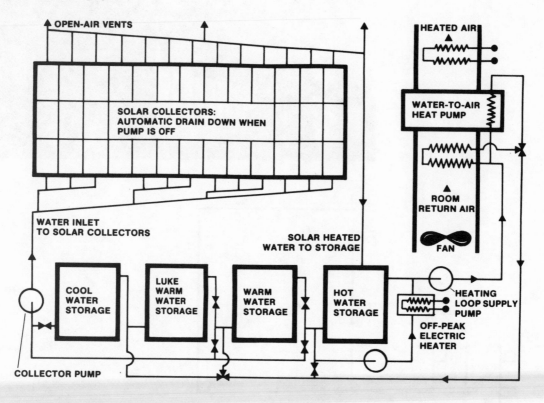

Active Solar Water-Heating System

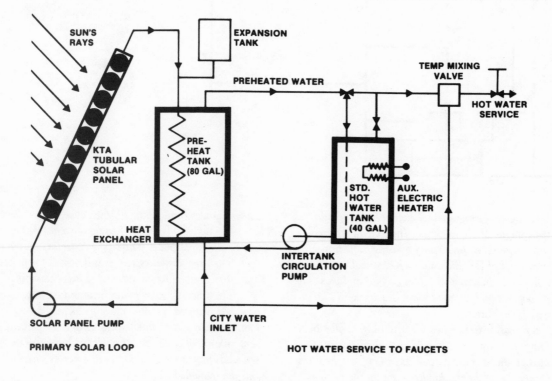

Ryland's Solar Demonstrations: A Tale of Two Houses

When The Ryland Group Inc. of Columbia, Maryland, built six active solar research houses in subdivisions in the Baltimore area in 1977, the company was interested in two kinds of research, said Ryland's in-house architect Don Taylor. Experimenting with solar and involving subcontractors in the research project was one goal. The other was to see what buyers thought about production-built solar housing.

The six active solar research homes were adaptions of one of Ryland's standard two-story models (shown below). Of course, the roof pitch was changed to accommodate the solar collectors.

The solar systems were expected to provide 70 percent of the heat and hot water for the 1728-square-foot homes. The systems, however, were not monitored for active solar contribution or savings.

The initial research results were interesting, although the active solar program was dropped by Ryland later.

First, the project showed, Taylor said, that subs could handle a pre-assembled, packaged, active solar system. Scientific Atlanta Inc., a solar manufacturer, supplied the hardware for three of the research houses. In addition, Ryland's subs showed they could fabricate a workable active solar system from off-the-shelf hardware. Medallion Industries Inc. designed and installed the solar systems on the other three houses.

Active Solar House

To get first-hand experience with active solar systems and to see what buyers thought about solar housing, The Ryland Group Inc. of Columbia, Maryland, built six active solar research houses in 1977 like the one shown here. With a few minor modifications, a standard Ryland model plan was used for the active solar demonstration homes. A front and rear elevation are shown.

Passive Solar House

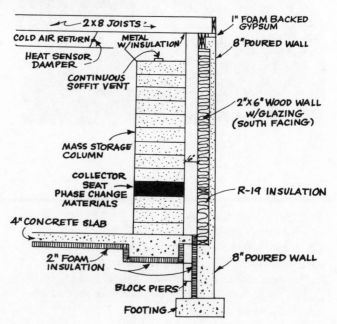

The 1756-square-foot, passive solar production house built by The Ryland Group of Columbia, Maryland, in 1980 will be monitored for two years to determine actual payback periods on its energy-saving features. The front of the house faces north.

The rear of the passive solar house faces south to maximize natural heat gain from the sun. The basement serves as headquarters for three passive solar systems. A deck provides an overhang to reduce heat gain in summer.

The schematic shows the construction details of the basement which serves for the collection, storage, and distribution of passive solar heat.

2X8 JOISTS

COLD AIR RETURN

HEAT SENSOR DAMPER

METAL W/INSULATION

CONTINUOUS SOFFIT VENT

1" FOAM BACKED GYPSUM

8" POURED WALL

2"X6" WOOD WALL W/GLAZING (SOUTH FACING)

MASS STORAGE COLUMN

COLLECTOR SEAT PHASE CHANGE MATERIALS

6"

R-19 INSULATION

4" CONCRETE SLAB

2" FOAM INSULATION

8" POURED WALL

BLOCK PIERS

FOOTING

SECOND FLOOR

M BRM
16'-8" x 12'-9"

BRM 3
10'-8" x 10'-11"

BRM 2
13'-0" x 10'-11"

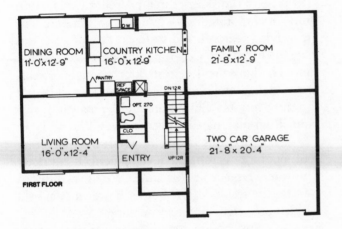

FIRST FLOOR

DINING ROOM
11'-0" x 12'-9"

COUNTRY KITCHEN
16'-0" x 12'-9"

FAMILY ROOM
21'-8" x 12'-9"

PANTRY

REF SPACE

DN 12 R

OPT. 270

CLO

LIVING ROOM
16'-0" x 12'-4"

ENTRY

UP 12R

TWO CAR GARAGE
21'-8" x 20'-4"

Note the vestibule air-lock entry to reduce air infiltration on the north side of the house. The plan was adapted from a standard model with few minor modifications, such as the vestibule entry.

A detailed drawing shows how the passive solar system works in winter and summer. In winter, heat from the sun is absorbed, stored, and distributed throughout the house. In summer, the deck above the basement windows shades the glazed areas to prevent overheating.

A shot of the basement shows the three columns that contain eutectic salts for storage and absorption of solar heat gain. Note that the heat from the columns can be distributed throughout the house through the ducting (at the top of the photo).

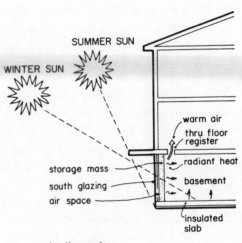

SUMMER SUN

WINTER SUN

warm air
thru floor
register

radiant heat

basement

storage mass

south glazing

air space

insulated
slab

heating cycle:
sun → storage mass → living space

Buyer reaction, in part, was predictable, initially. Solar does attract curiosity seekers. Traffic at some of the subdivisions, as a result, increased about twenty-fold when the active solar research houses opened, Taylor said.

To get a better feel for what buyers thought about the active solar systems, Ryland had prospects complete a questionnaire about the research homes. Early survey returns seemed to show that while many buyers were interested in active solar—more than 90 percent said that solar has promise and that they would consider purchasing a solar home—few would be willing to pay the price that Ryland would now have to charge for a solar house.

Asked how much additional they would be willing to spend for solar, only one in twenty who completed the questionnaire said a $12,000 to $14,000 price tag for active solar was acceptable. That only 5 percent would spend that much was important, because the active solar systems installed on Ryland's research houses cost on the average of $13,000 a piece, Taylor said.

Other survey results showed that some 63 percent of the respondents said they would spend an additional $8,000 to $10,000 for a solar heating system. In addition, more than 50 percent of the respondents said they would spend $1,200 to $1,400 for a solar water heating system.

But while many consumers indicated they would be willing to pay more for a solar system, in actuality, they were not willing to spend the extra for solar, said Ryland's marketing executive Robert Hafer. "There is a big difference what a survey says and what the consumer actually does," he said.

Although a lot of interest was shown in the active solar houses, Ryland had to lower the prices on the houses and take a loss to actually sell the houses. "We became disillusioned with the active solar program," he added.

But to further Ryland's research and interest in the future of solar systems in residential housing applications, The Ryland Group Inc. built a passive solar production house in 1980 to determine energy savings.

The Ryland passive solar demonstration model will be monitored for two years to evaluate realistic payback periods for energy-saving features.

Initial operation of the house from mid-December 1980 to mid-January 1981 showed a 50 percent to 60 percent savings when compared with a standard model. The monthly utility bill was about $100. Payback will begin to be calculated after about one year of actual operation.

With a grant from the National Institute of Building Sciences, the two-story, 1756-square-foot house will be monitored by the research foundation of the National Association of Home Builders and the Department of Energy.

The $108,000, three-bedroom production house incorporated about fifty-nine different energy-saving features and systems. "A lot of extras were included for experimental purposes," Hafer said. The house will be tested for a couple of years and, if the savings continue, the model will be put into production. "But we are pretty far away at this point from making that decision yet," he said.

"The house is not being used as a marketing tool, but for research and development. It is strictly a research project at this time. We are willing to wait for the results." The house, however, was sold within forty-eight hours of opening.

In transforming a standard model into a passive solar demonstration house, Ryland spent about $8,000 to $10,000 extra, Hafer said. That cost included construction of a deck on the rear elevation and a preheat device that uses heat from the heat pump to preheat water for the water heater.

Ryland also increased insulation on the house. Exterior walls were 24-inch on center to allow for more insulation, providing an R17 insulation value in the walls. The entire house was wrapped in a non-woven material that acts as an air infiltration barrier. Pipes and ducts were also wrapped in insulation. Two-inch-thick, plastic foam insulation was used to insulate footings and beneath the four-inch-thick, concrete basement slab. One inch of plastic foam insulation was used around the entire slab perimeter.

A tile floor in the basement lies on four inches of poured concrete and two inches of insulation in order to retain passive solar direct-heat gain. The floor absorbs the sun's heat as it enters through south-facing glass doors and windows. The concrete is expected to store heat for twelve hours in mild seasons and for six hours in cold weather. Heat is radiated through the house from seven floor registers.

Three concrete columns in the basement also collect heat and transfer it to the heating system's cold air return duct. The columns contain eutectic salts, a chemical storage material, run the length of the basement windows. They absorb the direct heat gain and transfer it into the heat duct system through a soffit in the basement ceiling. A dual-compressor heat pump supplements the passive solar heat in cold weather and provides air conditioning on hot days.

Other energy-saving features included: a vestibule entry to reduce air infiltration; vertical wiring to cut down on heat loss due to convection currents; closets located against exterior walls; rooftop ridge vents; and insulation wrapped around the water heater.

Windows on the north side of the house were triple-glazed and windows on the south side were specified as double-glazed. The sliding glass doors on the south side of the house were also double-glazed. The windows, doors, and rooms are being monitored for temperature, heat retention, and operation of the heat pump. Monitoring was provided by NAHB and the federal government.

Ryland expects to begin building houses of this type after about two years of testing, Hafer said. "We are concerned with the costs and selling price of the passive solar home as a production builder," he said. "But we are excited about passive. It is within our own means of construction."

Passive Solar Demonstration House: An Education for the Public and Builder Alike

A passive solar demonstration house cannot only educate the public about energy and provide valuable technical experience for the builder, it can also enhance a builder's image in the community.

"We're wearing white hats," said builder Doyle Stuckey of Houston, Texas. He completed a passive solar house in October 1980 in conjunction with the Southern Solar Energy Center, a regional office funded by the Department of Energy, and Environment Associates, an architectural firm.

Stuckey was surprised at the public's response to the project. In the first six weeks of an open house, four thousand people toured the home. "The streets were jammed with traffic," Stuckey said. "We have never seen such a response. They are sincerely concerned about reducing energy bills."

But that concern expressed itself in more than crowds and community image. The 2100-square-foot, demonstration home sold for $98,000 before completion and was constructed for about $42 per square foot excluding land. Four additional passive solar designs were also sold as a result in the custom development and others were put on the drawing board.

The experience of constructing the passive solar model made everyone in his organization more knowledgeable about passive solar, Stuckey felt. Also he felt that in addition to valuable technical knowledge, he has more confidence himself than he had before in passive solar. Stuckey said that the actual construction experience helped him see for himself how proper planning in construction can conserve energy. It was like seeing the results of a diet, he said.

Some of those measures were the proper use of insulation, placement of glass, reduction of air infiltration by stopping-up the cracks, and an increase in air movement through use of a ceiling fan instead of depending entirely on air conditioning.

In the model, passive solar construction averaged about 10 percent more per square foot, Stuckey said, but it was expected to save about 50 percent on heating and cooling bills. And instead of having to include a five-ton heat pump for heating and cooling, the reduced load in the house meant that he only had to install a two-ton unit.

Passive solar features in the model included: masonry mass to absorb the heat of the winter sun and store coolness at night during the summer; shading in summer through use of canopies over the windows; a ridge vent; and controlled flow of air through the high ceiling, causing a chimney effect. The interior of the house was designed so that cool air is drawn in and warm air is exhausted,

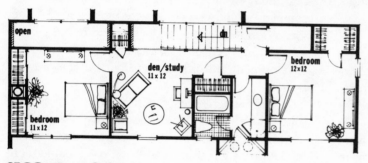

SECOND FLOOR

The photograph and floor plan show some of the passive solar features of Stuckey's demonstration house. Special attention was paid to natural cooling, due to the house's location in Houston, Texas. Note the shading devices on the exterior elevation which were designed to help keep the house cooler under the hot summer sun. For an open house, public viewers jammed the streets to tour the house. The house sold before completion for $98,000 in October 1980.

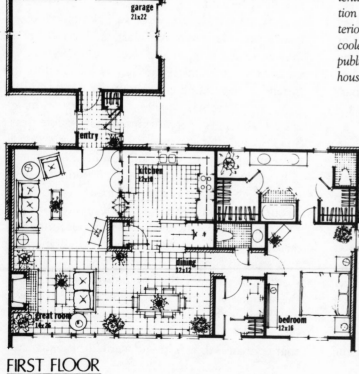

FIRST FLOOR

Passive Solar Features for Heating and Cooling

Movable overhang shades first floor windows when
    needed
Fixed overhangs control solar exposure on second floor
Masonry floors to store solar heat in winter and cool in
    summer
Brick interior walls store heating and cooling
Site orientation for proper solar exposure
Insulation
Tight shell construction for infiltration control
Vestibule and laundry room serve as entry air locks
Double-glazed thermal windows

Passive Solar Features for Heating Exclusively

Passive direct solar heat gain in winter
Garage located on northeast side of house to protect
    living spaces from cold winter winds

Passive Solar Features for Cooling Exclusively

Reflective glazing on east wall
Window design for cross ventilation
High clerestory window over kitchen and dining area
    vents out excess heat
Vented west wall with no windows rejects summer heat
Attic fan ventilation
Ridge and soffit attic venting
Radiant barrier in roof rejects summer heat

SOURCE: Southern Solar Energy Center.

an important consideration for southern climates in the summer months. An airspace between the roof deck and the insulation allows the air to be drawn through. The house also included R19-insulated ceiling, R13-insulated walls, and an insulated slab foundation.

Stuckey noted that the public was very responsive to passive solar. "It is not whether people would prefer passive solar or not," he said. "They would like it, but most of them can't afford it."

In his conventional houses, Stuckey used trial and error experience over a period of about four or five years to develop an energy conservation package, including monitoring some actual houses. He estimated that the energy packages, which vary by project, cost about 2 to 3 percent of the cost of the house. He found that a few lending agencies take those extra costs into consideration when qualifying buyers.

But consumers are the ones who must be convinced that energy saving houses are cost-effective, Stuckey said. "There is a limit to what they will pay for . . . and afford." But as in the automobile industry, Stuckey pointed out, an energy-efficient house will appreciate more in value than a comparable conventional house with less regard to payback. "It is simply more valuable in comparison," he said.

Chicago Solar Demo: Big Downtime, Big Repair Costs and a Big Disappointment

The residential solar demonstration program sponsored by the Department of Housing and Urban Development in the late 1970s produced many solar successes. It also produced some less successful projects; and it left a lot of lessons to be learned.

It's a good thing, for example, that four active solar-heated, demonstration townhouses in suburban Chicago had a backup heating system, because cold weather and system failure shut down solar operations for much of the winter of 1977.

In an effort to prove that active solar energy was practical for production housing in Chicago, United Development Co. constructed four solar-heated townhouses in 1976 in its suburban Chicago New Century Town development. The townhouses were among the first units completed and field-tested under HUD's solar demonstration program. The test results were disappointing to say the least.

Upon completion of the units, the townhomes were rented and expected to be monitored for performance of the solar systems for a period of two years. But downtime for repairs and modifications of the solar system was so extended that United Development Co. really could not even get a good idea as to how well the system would work, said company president Robert Frommer.

The performance of the demonstration solar system with roof-mounted collectors installed on four town-houses at United Development Company's New Century Town near Chicago in 1977 was disappointing. Builder Frommer, however, labeled it a "learning experience."

If things went as planned, the solar system was supposed to provide up to 60 percent of the heat and most of the hot water for the townhouses. But during the winter of 1977, fuel bills in the solar-heated townhouses were no lower than fuel bills in similar, conventionally built townhouses in New Century Town.

The expected performance would have represented a sizable savings in operating costs for the homeowner. But even then, the payback period was lengthy in light of the extra initial costs of $12,000 per unit for installation of each of the solar systems. In 1977, the conventionally heated two and three bedroom townhouses sold for $40,500 to $54,300.

That high a premium for solar energy makes it a less than feasible alternative right now, said Frommer in the design stage of the project—before the problems set in. But the firm undertook the project under the assumption that first costs for solar would decrease and conventional fuel prices would continue to increase.

A solar system was selected on the basis that it would be applicable to conventional housing and simple enough for installation and maintenance by tradespeople with no special training.

To accommodate the solar collectors, the pitch of the south-facing roofs was increased over those of conventionally designed units. The only other major change required by the solar installation was the use of insulation around the foundation which would minimize heat loss in the 1000-gallon, basement tank to store water heated by the collectors. Supplemental heat was designed to be supplied by a water-to-water heat pump that would automatically switch on and extract what heat was available from the storage tank. If the water in the tank was not hot enough (due to prolonged cloudiness, for example), additional backup heat would be provided by an oversized gas-fired hot water tank.

It sounded simple enough. But in actual operation, the solar system was surrounded by a multitude of problems. Among them were: freeze-ups, leaks, compression failures, excessive operation of the heat pump system, and poor performance of a reflective roof. The company expected some problems, Frommer said, but nobody expected the problems to persist and new problems to pop up after a brief shake-down period.

The necessary repairs and modifications were costly, adding about $14,000 to the $56,000 actual first cost of the solar system for the four townhome units, Frommer said. HUD provided a $40,000 subsidy under the solar demonstration program to help cover costs.

The most expensive repair of $6,000 involved replacing the original white, asphalt-shingled roof with a white, vinyl-coated aluminum roof. The new roof was meant to increase reflection to the back of the newly developed Owens-Illinois collectors that were used on the townhouses.

United Development Co. rented three of the four townhouses. When the solar system was out of operation during two winter months, the company actually paid the residents' heating bills. Nonetheless, the occupants complained about the performance of the solar system, and local newspapers picked up on the complaints, calling the experiment a failure.

But Frommer disagreed. To him, it was not a failure; it was a learning experience. "What we attempted to do during this first phase was to develop a reliable solar heating system," he said. "We were looking for problems. We found them."

Along with technical developments, solar design has progressed as well, making solar aesthetically pleasing and efficient. The solarium of this house in Seattle, Washington, serves as a passive solar heat collector and a functional living area.

3

DEVELOPMENT OF SOLAR DESIGN

There was a time when anyone could spot a solar house a mile away. Collector panels tacked on a roof could be an eyesore. But eventually it took a closer look. Although active solar collector panels still appear on roofs, they are being integrated into the actual roof structure and slope. And some solar houses are not obvious at all. The panels now appear on side walls and flat roof parapets, all designed to collect solar energy, not stares.

Some builders found that they could integrate solar easily into their standard model plans with minor modifications. Others designed the houses entirely with solar in mind.

But a solar house is not all that meets the eye. Don Watson, an architect from Guilford, Connecticut, feels that an active solar energy system should come last in a series of energy-saving steps. First, he said, builders should winterize the house to reduce its heating requirements. Second, they should incorporate passive solar design features such as southern exposure, double-glazed windows for winter heat gain, insulating shades, and overhangs for summer shading. These items do not necessarily cost much more, Watson said. The last step would be an active solar system designed for the particular region. Only then can an active solar system be energy efficient, he said. "Passive design principles can improve energy savings without raising the cost of the home," Watson said.

Architect and builder Ralph Brill of Brill, Kawakami, Wilborne in Cold Spring, New York, also considers the collectors only a small part of a total solar system. A believer in passive solar features such as greenhouses for heat gain and natural ventilation, Brill designed all of his houses with at least solar "potential" (piping installed) for possible future use. Brill suggests that for a marketable solar home, builders should "marry technology and aesthetics."

Many builders like Brill turned to active solar systems in the search for a more energy-efficient house. For builder R.B. Fitch of Carrboro, North Carolina, solar was a natural progression on his road of energy savers. Fitch wanted a solar system that he could put together himself to control production and costs. So, for one of his houses, he designed and built his own with the help of engineers. The panels were constructed on-site and took the place of siding on one exterior wall. Far from looking "home-made," the panels blended with the house design.

Other builders use architecture to hide the collector panels. Amrep Corp., builder of the Rio Rancho development near Albuquerque, New Mexico, hid the collectors in a roof parapet "well" of a solar spec house. Interest was so strong, "even the competition came to see it," one company official said.

A custom house can take advantage of incorporating active solar into the house design. In Cold Spring, New York, this $200,000 custom house contained a $9,000 Sunworks solar system to provide 65 percent of the heating needs. Other features included passive solar design ideas such as southern-exposure glass areas for direct heat gain, a natural ventilation system, insulation, and orienting the house to the sun and wind. Completed in the spring of 1977, the house was designed by Ralph Brill of Brill, Kawakami, Wilborne, and built by D. Yannetelli.

Vertical active solar collector panels, constructed on-site by builder R.B. Fitch of Carrboro, North Carolina, took the place of siding on one exterior wall. The system was designed to provide 60 to 80 percent of the space heat and hot water for the 1400-square-foot house. SOURCE: American Plywood Association.

Amrep Corp., developers of Rio Rancho near Albuquerque, New Mexico, created a flat-roof "well" to hide active solar collectors on a modified model in 1977. Manufactured and installed by Solar Seven Industries, the $9,000 active solar system, including extra insulation in each home, provided about 75 percent of the heat and 90 percent of the water-heating needs.

A flat-roof parapet helps disguise the active solar installation on these houses built by Warren Buckmaster of Hemet, California. A combination of insulation and the Revere active solar system provided over 90 percent of the heating requirements for the 1000- to 1500-square-foot homes. The houses ranged in price from $43,000 to $52,400 in 1977.

Warren Buckmaster, a builder from Hemet, California, had a similar idea. But instead of creating a "well" on the roof like Amrep Corp., Buckmaster hid collectors in a flat roof parapet. The flat roof provided the flexibility to adapt the Revere collectors to the houses' orientation, an important consideration in a tract development. A combination of insulation and the active solar system provided over 90 percent of the heating requirements for the 1000 to 1500 square-foot homes. "I probably made and corrected every mistake in the book," Buckmaster said about the development of his solar system. The basic concept behind the hidden collectors was to create marketable solar homes, Buckmaster said. He knew that solar houses initially drew large crowds. Crowds are one thing, but will they buy? Buckmaster questioned at first. But he found that experience encouraged sales. Buckmaster found buyers in 1977 curious but reluctant at

first. Yet in his second phase of solar tract homes, the hesitancy was gone and all of the houses were sold in the framing stage.

Architect Barry Berkus also sought a way to hide active solar collectors within architecture without reducing efficiency. Similar to the Amrep and Buckmaster ideas, Berkus hid the collectors in a flat roof parapet in a development of four $200,000 solar spec houses in 1977. Berkus used strong roof forms to make the most of the surrounding environment of a steep-grade, hillside site overlooking Santa Barbara, California. In encouraging buyers to consider solar homes, Berkus said that the proof for buyers is in the bills. He found that buyers of his custom solar homes showed pride in their low energy bills. That was one of the best persuaders of all to buy.

Solar houses attract a lot of attention from the public and the media and draw big crowds,

Architect Barry Berkus sought a way to hide the solar collectors into the architecture without reducing efficiency. He located the solar collectors in a flat-roof parapet, not visible from street level (aerial view shown) in a development of four $200,000 spec houses. In the 2500-square-foot house, the $9,500 Era del Sol active solar system provided about 50 percent of the heat and 100 percent of the water-heating needs. The houses were completed in 1977.

In the face of large, expensive custom solar homes, builder Jerry Verthein of Baraboo, Wisconsin proved that solar can work on a small, 1000-square-foot house. The house was completed in July 1977. Construction cost including solar was $38.90 per square foot. The solar system provided about 80 percent of the house's heating requirements.

according to many builders. As others found, the crowds are not always just curiosity seekers, said builder Jerry Verthein of Baraboo, Wisconsin. Verthein's solar house, built in 1977 through the HUD residential solar demonstration program, drew three times the traffic of an ordinary model. Verthein's slant on solar construction was to fit the system on a small house without overpowering it. He adapted a Sun Stone solar system to the rear elevation of a 1000-square-foot, three-bedroom standard model. An identical house without solar was built across the street. In comparison, the solar system provided about 80 percent of the heating requirements. With electric baseboard heating, the non-solar house received a typical bill of about $150 in the winter of 1977–1978. In the same winter period, the solar house heating bill was only $30.

In some markets, like Verthein's, buyers seem to feel more comfortable with standard models that are adapted to solar than with new architectural styles. To increase the marketability of solar homes, Alpha Construction Co. of Canton, Ohio, adapted solar to one of their traditional standard models. The company officials noticed that most of the solar homes that they saw were contemporary, but their current market was mostly interested in traditional homes. But in addition to building traditional-style solar designs, they wanted to prove that active solar systems could work in an area with cold weather and cloud cover.

In other markets, particularly custom installations, just about anything goes. For something completely different, architect Charles A. Haertling designed a passive and active solar custom home which revolved around two reinforced-block, cylindrical towers. One tower enclosed the mechanical systems for the solar. The other held the staircase. As a maverick, Haertling saw his role as trying new things with solar, he said. He was

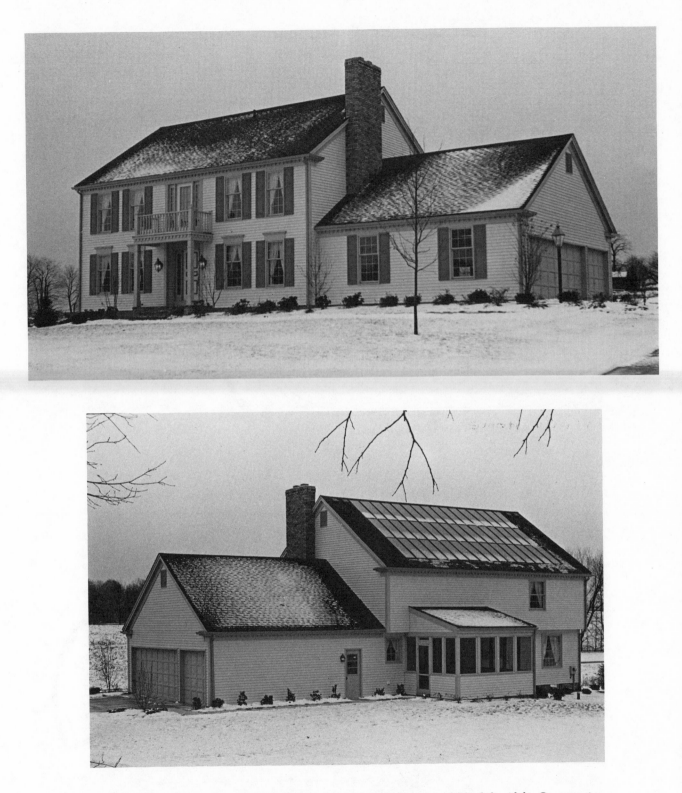

Solar can be adapted to a traditional standard plan, as shown in this model built by Alpha Construction Co. of Canton, Ohio. The active solar system was designed to provide 50 percent of the space heat and 70 percent of the water-heating needs, using Rom-Aire solar collectors and heavy insulation (R20 walls and R36 ceiling). The house was completed and sold in 1977.

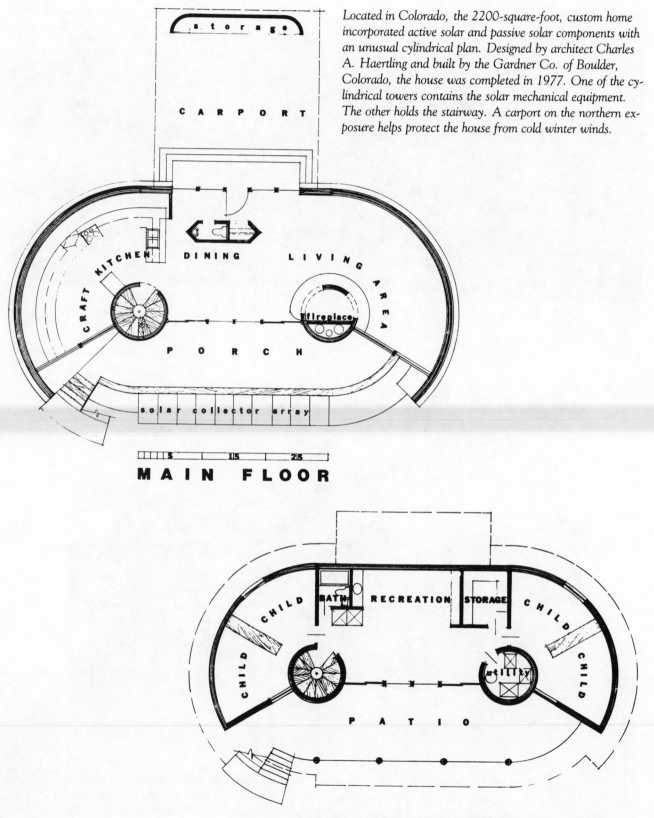

Located in Colorado, the 2200-square-foot, custom home incorporated active solar and passive solar components with an unusual cylindrical plan. Designed by architect Charles A. Haertling and built by the Gardner Co. of Boulder, Colorado, the house was completed in 1977. One of the cylindrical towers contains the solar mechanical equipment. The other holds the stairway. A carport on the northern exposure helps protect the house from cold winter winds.

storage

CARPORT

CRAFT KITCHEN

DINING

LIVING AREA

fireplace

PORCH

solar collector array

5 15 25

MAIN FLOOR

CHILD CHILD

BATH

RECREATION

STORAGE

CHILD CHILD

utility

PATIO

GROUND FLOOR

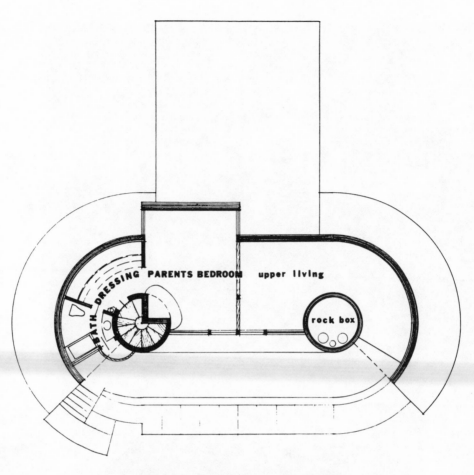

BALCONY FLOOR

Builder and designer Harry Wenning of LaGrange, New York, received one of the first HUD solar grants to construct this 4000-square-foot house. Passive solar features, such as southern exposure windows with insulating automatic drapes and a Revere active solar system, provided about 75 percent of the heat and about 90 percent of the water-heating requirements. Extra space was left on the roof for future installation of photovoltaic panels.

interested in experimenting with solar research, including passive components, integral greenhouse, remote solar collectors, and houses with solar potential for later installation. "Solar will be necessary in the future," he said, "but I'm an architect, not Buck Rogers." In his 1977 custom house, he incorporated a more comprehensive approach to solar. The solar systems were designed integrally with the architecture. The house was designed totally to accommodate solar and protect it from the wind, he said. Overhangs served as an architectural element as well as a passive solar component for summer shading.

Some builders oriented their houses with large glazed areas, provided correct roof pitch, and included duct-work or piping for future solar installations. Other builders built solar houses with future technology in mind. In November 1976, builder and designer Harry Wenning of LaGrange, New York, completed a 4000-square-foot passive and active solar house with 1200 square feet of flat-plate solar collectors for space heat and hot water located on a south-facing roof slope. It was designed to provide about 75 percent of the heat and 90 percent of the hot water requirements. But on the roof, Wenning also provided room for future photovoltaic panels when they become economically feasible. The house, built with one of the first HUD solar grants, sold for about $189,000 in 1977 on a two-acre site. Wenning estimated that the solar system added about $5 per square foot to the cost of the home.

Like the other builders mentioned previously, Wenning included passive solar techniques such as increased insulation, south-facing windows, and roof overhangs. Then active solar was added. Wenning had designed about two hundred passive solar homes before his interest in active solar systems was sparked. "I stopped talking, and started building," he said.

Houses are becoming more functional out of need. Increased construction and land costs have sent many builders back to the drawing board to make the most of every square foot of land and living space. The results are smaller and more efficient houses and higher densities. But while more functional, designs are still eye-appealing and marketable.

But just as the designs have been adapted for land and construction cost efficiencies while retaining aesthetic appeal, solar house design is becoming less noticeable and more attractive. Passive solar energy principles, for instance, also combine function and aesthetics. Features such as sunspaces and greenhouses help heat the house while making the house more desirable to live in. The difference between function and aesthetics is becoming harder and harder to distinguish.

A solar house does not have to look like a solar house. Poor building appearance is an unnecessary barrier to marketable solar homes. Although housing design must cater to the incorporation of an active or passive solar system, it must also cater to the aesthetics and lifestyle needs of the buyers. A solar system is simply designed to increase the homeowner's thermal comfort. It should also be pleasing to the buyer's eye.

Passive Solar: Perfect for a Non-Residential Renovation

Passive solar design principles are not just limited to residential applications. In many cases, they can work even better in non-residential buildings.

"Passive solar is perfect for commercial space," said Milton Sandy Jr., president of M.L. Sandy Lumber Sales Co. Inc. in Corinth, Mississippi. "It doesn't require storage because the area is basically only used when the sun is shining," he pointed out. "The area is not occupied twenty-four hours a day as in a residential application."

Sandy renovated an old, abandoned service station in late 1980 into retail space. The total renovation cost, including a $750 passive solar bead wall, was about $10 per square foot. He said that compared with about $30 per square foot in construction costs if he had demolished the building and constructed a new one. "The structure was too sound to tear down," he said. "But aesthetically it was unusable."

The 2500 square feet of space were renovated for a total cost of $25,000. The old glass sales area was torn down due to its deteriorated condition and replaced by a new, 560-square-foot, frame structure

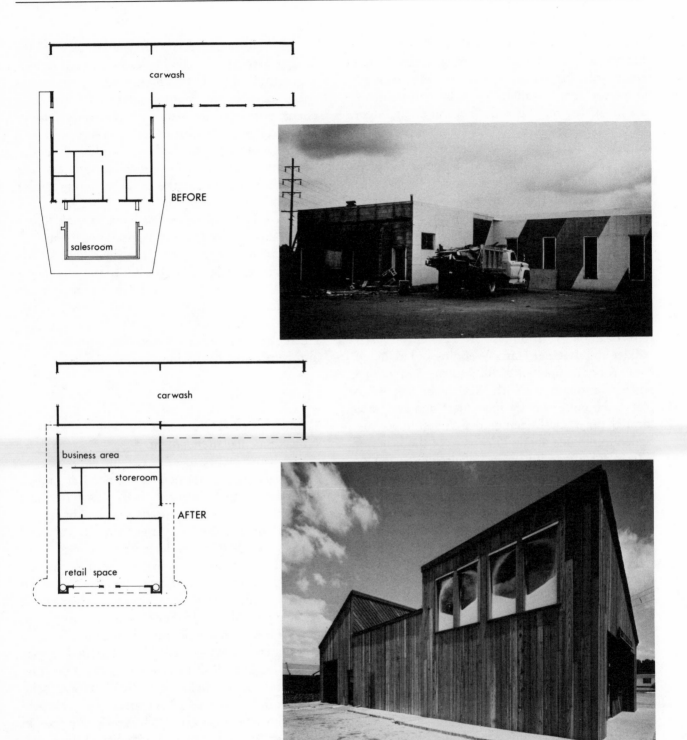

The before and after photographs and plans show the dramatic difference in the renovation of the old, abandoned service station into retail shops. The glass-enclosed sales room (see before plan) was demolished and replaced by a retail space constructed on the same concrete slab. PHOTOS: Hursley & Lark/ California Redwood Association. Floor plans courtesy of M.L. Sandy, Corinth, Mississippi.

During renovation, pre-engineered roof trusses were added for architectural appeal and to provide the opportunity for clerestory windows for direct passive solar heat gain.

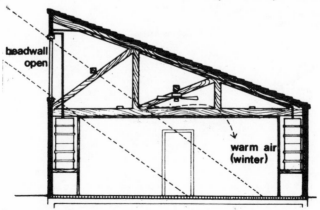

The diagram shows how the sunlight penetrates into the building during winter days when the bead wall is open. On winter nights and summer days, the bead wall is filled for insulation in winter and shading in summer. A ceiling fan aids in the redistribution of heat in winter and cooling in summer.

on the old slab. The whole building was divided into three basic areas, currently occupied by a package liquor store and a car restoration shop.

Pre-engineered roof trusses were added to make the building more attractive. But they also provided the opportunity to include a south-facing clerestory window in the retail area for passive solar heat gain. The roof angle over the car wash tunnel is adaptable for future use of active solar heating.

The clerestory window is comprised of glass salvaged from the old glass sales area which was demolished. The double-glazed window includes a three-inch air space between glass panes in which Styrofoam beads are pumped automatically for insulation at night and pumped out again during the day to make the most of natural heat gain. The system is reversed in the summer when shading is needed during the day. The bead wall is automati-

cally controlled by a thermostat, which, Sandy said, takes the responsibility for the system operation off the shoulders of the tenant.

The clerestory windows were designed for natural illumination as well as direct solar heat gain in winter. But in the southern climate, Sandy realized they required shading in summer to avoid problems of overheating the interior space. The bead wall was a simple and low-cost solution for summer shading as well as insulating on winter nights, he said. Ceiling fans were also included to help redistribute heat in the winter and cooling in summer.

The added cost of the bead wall included the 55-gallon storage drums for the beads, valves, cost of the plans designed by the Zomeworks Corp., vacuum cleaner motor, and PVC pipe between the tank and windows.

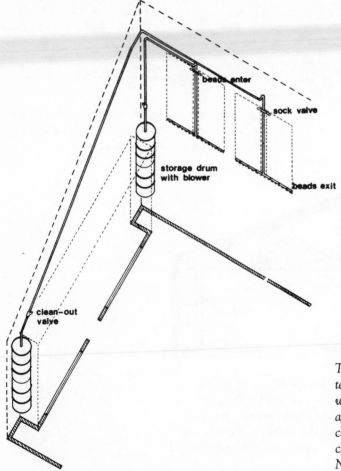

beads enter

sock valve

storage drum
with blower

beads exit

clean-out
valve

The schematic drawing shows how Sandy's bead wall system works. Styrofoam beads are pumped in and out of the window cavity through PVC pipes and into 55-gallon storage drums. The system is powered by an ordinary vacuum cleaner motor. The system plans and instructions were purchased by Sandy from Zomeworks Corp. of Albuquerque, New Mexico.

In addition, for energy efficiency, an insulation sandwich was created by applying 1½-inch furring strips to the exterior of the concrete block structure with one-inch foam insulation board between the strips and covered with redwood siding. Sandy kept the concrete mass *inside* the building for thermal efficiency.

Backup heat is supplied by a combination split heating and cooling system which is smaller than typically specified for this size building due to the passive solar contribution. But even that was more than necessary. During the entire winter of 1980–1981, the backup heating system was needed for only a total of two hours during the Christmas Eve rush when a large volume of customers kept the doors open too long. Sandy noted that the building was more efficient than first realized. The building even traps the heat from the store's cooler compressor.

The initial costs for the passive solar components are a trade-off, Sandy said. He did not calculate payback or estimated savings. "The operating costs are less," he said, "and it will pay-back forever." In addition, the experience of building solar in itself was worth it, he said. This was Sandy's second passive-solar, non-residential application.

Passive solar will also add to the future saleability of the building, he noted, and possibly will allow him to command a higher rent due to reduced utility costs to the tenants.

Sandy also pointed out that a liquor store tenant is perfect for a passive solar building. "The liquor bottles tend to retain heat," he said. "They are a perfect storage device."

When Sandy purchased the building for investment, it was "a vacant eyesore," he said. Although the building was located at the busiest intersection in town, the flat roof leaked and the car wash tunnel did not match the rest of the building. For aesthetics, in addition to the new roof trusses, a new exterior skin was applied, consisting of a knotty rustic grade of redwood. "It was very economical wood siding," Sandy said. The economies of using a less expensive grade of redwood helped make the project feasible.

Because the project was located in a very visible location, Sandy wanted to try something different and use products in creative ways for a retail area. He printed a small brochure to help expose the public to the passive solar design principles used in the building. It states right at the top, "Solar can be simple."

Building a Solar, Manufactured House: Experience Comes in the Package

Many solar houses have been designed and constructed by trial and error. A builder learns through experience. That is one big advantage of building a manufactured pre-cut solar house, according to Richard Neroni, general manager of Timberpeg, which designs and manufactures post-and-beam, pre-cut houses. "The education has already been done," he said. "The advantage for builders is the availability of engineered solar designs which take the trial and error out of constructing a solar house."

In 1980, Timberpeg introduced four solar plans: two passive solar models, one hybrid house (combining passive and active solar energy systems), and one active solar plan, ranging from 790 square feet to 1992 square feet of living space. The pre-cut packages are manufactured in Timberpeg's plants in Claremont, New Hampshire, and Elkin, North Carolina.

The solar houses were designed to combine post-and-beam construction with solar considerations. Estimated solar contribution ranged from about 40 to 70 percent, depending on the climatic region and the house design.

One advantage of using post-and-beam construction in a solar house was the benefit of an uninterrupted envelope of insulation surrounding the house, Neroni said. In the solar houses, three inches of Thermax foam sheathing was sandwiched between interior wall materials, a 1 × 4 grid for an air space, and the exterior siding materials. All of the coverings were applied to the exterior of the beam construction, eliminating air infiltration which occurs through studs in conventionally built houses. The solar houses included one inch more insulation than the standard Timberpeg designs. The walls and ceilings of the solar houses were insulated to R30. The standard Timberpeg plans include R23 wall insulation and R22 ceiling insulation. In addition, wood-framed Andersen Perma Shield windows were included as well as Peachtree wood-framed sliding patio doors. Each of the solar homes also included a centrally located wood stove and conventional backup heating system for supplemental heat.

In addition to the added insulation, passive solar features included:

- Minimization of exterior wall and roof surfaces by using compact house shapes to reduce heat loss;
- Triple-glazing of windows on the north, east, and west exposures to reduce heat loss;
- Exposed interior masonry in walls and floors to absorb and store direct solar heat gain;
- Open interior space between living levels to aid natural air convection;
- Air-lock double entries (in some plans) to reduce cold-air infiltration.

Neroni pointed out that proper siting of the houses maximizes the efficiency of the units. The Timberpeg designs were considered to be most efficient in the mid-Atlantic states, the Northeast, Midwest, and Rockies—regions where heating is the primary mode.

Solar features, of course, added to the cost of the home. In the passive solar plans, extra insulation and triple-glazed windows added to construction costs. In the active solar plan, collectors and other solar mechanical equipment added about an extra $10,000 to the initial cost of the home, according to Neroni.

But Neroni discovered that buyers were not as concerned about payback as might be expected. "They are purchasing the solar home because it is well-constructed, well-designed, and aesthetically attractive, and just happens to be solar," he said. "They like the house. Solar is just an added benefit to save energy and make the house more valuable. . . . All other things aside, solar will not induce them to buy," Neroni noted.

The most popular Timberpeg solar plan was the 1800-square-foot, three-bedroom passive solar model. The Solar III plan won a design competition sponsored by the Department of Energy. Built in Scranton, Pennsylvania, in 1980, the house provided 65 percent of the heating needs through passive solar energy. Passive solar energy was calculated to contribute 46 percent of the heating requirements if the house was located in Maine, 65 percent in Boston, 70 percent in Long Island, New York, and 75 percent in Washington, D.C.

In the Solar III plan, solar features included two passive solar collection areas (see floor plan on page 90). A one-story, four-foot by sixteen-foot greenhouse contained two sets of double-glazed wood sliding doors, two roof skylights, a paving-brick floor laid on a four-inch concrete slab to absorb and radiate solar heat, and an interior trombe wall. The twelve-inch-thick trombe wall, which separated the greenhouse from the kitchen/dining room, consisted of concrete block faced on both sides with brick. The heavy-mass masonry surface helps control wide swings in temperature by retaining solar heat gain and releasing it as the house cools down in the evening. Two double French doors in the wall provided natural light, view, and direct access to the greenhouse.

The second passive solar collection area was a two-story sunspace adjacent to the living room on the first floor and the master bedroom on the second floor. Because this area contains comparably little thermal mass, solar heat rises to the top of the sunspace and is distributed by air-handling equipment throughout the house as needed, or to an insulated rock bin in the foundation for storage. When heat is needed in the house, an automatic thermostat channels heat from the storage bin to the house. If not enough heat is supplied by solar storage, the backup heating system turns on automatically. Supplemental heat could also be supplied by the centrally located wood stove.

Overheating in the sunspace and greenhouse during the summer months was prevented by roof overhangs, optional louvered blinds, sliding patio doors for ventilation, and screened roof windows in the greenhouse.

In 1980, the basic house packages for the solar designs ranged from about $18,339 to $47,340. Cost of the completed structure, without land or site improvements, was estimated to reach

The front and rear elevations of the Timberpeg Solar III plan are shown. Glazed areas were minimized on the north, east, and west exposures and maximized on the southern exposure for optimum solar heat gain.

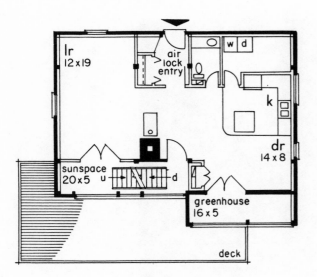

First Floor

The 1800-square-foot, passive-solar plan provided two areas for collection of solar heat: a sunspace and a greenhouse. It should be noted that due to the post-and-beam construction, all interior partition walls were non-loadbearing and could be moved per buyer specifications.

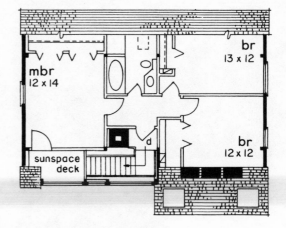

Second Floor

COMPARATIVE HEATING COSTS

Location	Electric Baseboard Heating @ 100% efficiency (7¢ per kilowatt hour)		Electric Furnace @ 80% Efficiency (In-duct Strip Heater)
	Conventional 2 × 4 stud house	Timberpeg Standard Gambrel	Timberpeg Solar III
Boston	$1370	$987	$266
Long Island, N.Y.	1119	802	174
Washington, D.C.	896	669	134

Comparative heating costs for a conventional gambrel house, a standard Timberpeg gambrel, and the Timberpeg solar gambrel are shown for three locations. The estimated space heating fuel costs were based on 1980 prices. SOURCE: Timberpeg.

A greenhouse in the Timberpeg Solar III model was used to collect, absorb, and radiate solar heat gain. The brick wall provided thermal mass to help retain solar heat.

from $38,000 to $140,000. The pre-cut building system, however, provided substantial savings by reducing construction time by about two to three weeks, compared with conventional stick-built houses. The savings in construction time could be used to offset the extra cost of the solar features.

Energy System Capitalizes on "Free" Elements

One way to reduce heating and cooling bills is to make the most of free energy. Custom builder Jesse Jones of Houston literally looked high and low for

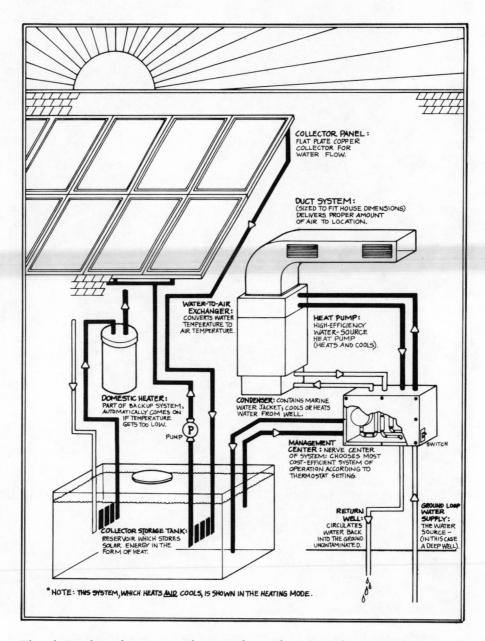

The solar/geothermal system uses the sun and ground water as "free" energy sources. Well water is circulated through a water source heat pump to temper air for heating or cooling. The solar system supplies heat for heating and hot water.

The Solarun model, built by Jesse Jones in the Woodlands, Texas, near Houston, is a solar house; but it also uses ground water to help cool the house in the summer. The $160,000 model was built without government aid.

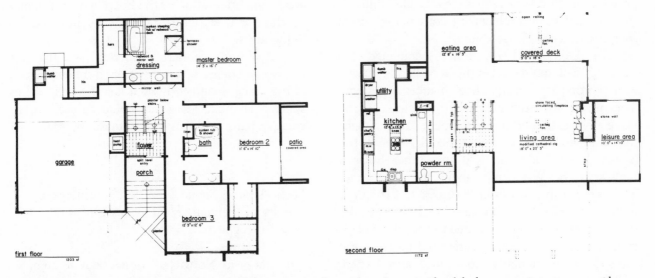

To help reduce direct heat gain in living areas, the garage was designed on the west side of the house, an important consideration in climates where cooling is the primary need.

the most efficient heating and cooling system that he could find. The result was an energy system which took advantage of what he called "two free commodities": the sun and ground water.

The system combined the benefits of solar heating with the long-known water source heat pump which uses well water to help heat and cool the house. The entire system was designed to cut utility bills in half.

Water in the 250-foot well remains at a constant 68 degrees Fahrenheit year-round. In winter the well water preheats the air used for heating. In summer, the water precools the air used for cooling (see schematic). Using a closed loop, the water is extracted from the ground and returned again after passing through the system.

In early 1979, the initial cost of the entire system was about $8,000 more than a conventional heating/cooling system, including the cost of the wells, solar collection system, backup water source heat pump, automatic controls to regulate the system, and a 1400-gallon, glass-fiber storage tank.

Jones found that most buyers initially balked at the cost of the system. But with the rising cost of utilities, Jones considers the system as equity in the home. "Equity does not require a payback period," Jones said. "The buyer will get his investment back when he sells the home." The system had an estimated five-year payback. Jones, though, tried also to stress immediate energy savings to his buyers rather than just long-term payback. He admitted that he had some problems in convincing buyers that energy savings was equity.

In October 1978, Jones completed his $160,000 Solarun model in the Woodlands, Texas, as a prototype for using "free" sources of energy. The model attracted plenty of attention. In the three months that it was open, about eight thousand to nine thousand people toured the house. Jones built and sold two other Solarun houses in the Woodlands about the same time. They ranged in price from $115,000 to $165,000, including a $25,000 golf course lot. Interest in the solar/geothermal system resulted in the sale of plans to about a dozen initially interested builders and individuals, particularly from rural areas where wells are common, Jones said.

Solar designer Wendell Dillard of Houston said that the homes save "an honest 50 percent" on utility bills. The system reportedly saved about 70 percent on heating costs and about 30 percent to 40 percent on cooling. In comparing two actual houses for one month of the cooling season near Houston in 1978, one conventional house had an electric bill of $143. The solar house, with 400 square feet more space, had a bill of $54.

The cost of the well was the most expensive part of the system, said Jones. But Dillard suggested that in a tract housing project, one well could be used to supply several homes with ground water, not just one.

Dillard claimed that the water source heat pump is more efficient than conventional heat pumps. The water source unit achieved a 13.3 Energy Efficient Rating, while conventional heat pumps generally were rated about a 7 or 8 EER.

In addition to the solar/geothermal system, the house was designed to make the most of energy conservation. Walls were insulated to R21, using a combination of cellulose fiber insulation, foil-backed foam wall sheathing, an air infiltration barrier, and wood siding. The attic insulation had an R30 rating.

Other energy savers included ceiling fans to circulate the air, a heat-circulating fireplace, attic power vents, covered porches, overhangs and sun baffles to protect glass from solar heat gain in living areas, and orientation of the house with the garage on the hot west side to reduce solar heat gain in living areas.

Architect Kenneth Anderson said that the additional energy savers functioned independently of the active solar/geothermal heating and cooling system. They are ideas that could be used in any energy saving house in that climate, he said.

Solar Armory Shows How to Cut Energy Use by 30 Percent: Heat Areas Only When Occupied

An armory in Norwich, Connecticut, is right on target for energy savings. Utilizing solar panels and energy-efficient design, the Norwich Armed Forces Reserve Center was designed to use less than 30 percent of the heat needed for a comparable building.

Designed by William H. Grover of Moore Grover Harper architects of Essex, Connecticut, the building's efficiency is inherent in its floor plan and structure. The building revolves around an "occupied/unoccupied" plan. The principle was to heat areas only when occupied. The 27,900-square-foot armory, 7,900-square-foot office area, and the 4,484-square-foot maintenance shop are the three main centers of the system.

The armory on the first floor is used only a few evenings and weekends per month. It relies solely on solar energy to maintain 55-degrees-plus when it is not in use. When occupied, an oil-fired furnace brings the armory up to a comfortable temperature.

Meanwhile, the offices which are used daily have their own array of active solar panels and south-facing windows to maintain a comfortable working climate. A 2000-gallon tank stores heat for the offices and provides hot water. A timed thermostat lowers the offices' temperature at night.

A vehicle maintenance shop was located in a separate building. Actual operating data showed

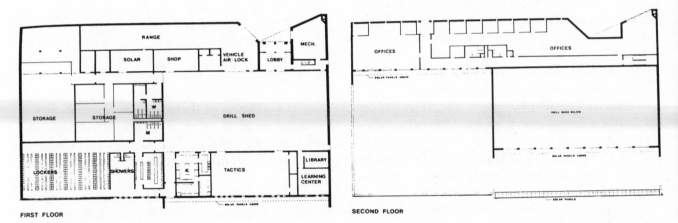

The floor plans were designed for heating of areas only when occupied. By retaining offices strictly on the second and separate floor, the first floor can be heated only when the area is needed. Entry and vehicle air locks also help save energy. The armory was designed by William H. Grover of Moore Grover Harper Architects.

The brick-veneered, concrete block armory was designed for energy efficiency and cost-efficient active and passive solar heat. The building was especially designed to heat areas only when occupied.

that it used only about 10 percent of the fuel needed to heat a comparable building. Architect Bill Grover pointed out that it is fairly easy to make comparisons since the square footage of armory installations remains fairly standard.

Since the buildings' completion in April 1978, the active solar system has performed up to expectations economically, Grover said. Actual savings are hard to calculate because the monitoring system for measuring the active solar contribution was not installed. The passive portion of the energy savings is difficult to measure, but the buildings are reported to be performing well.

A few initial problems were experienced with the active solar system and the heat exchanger, due to a leak caused by a silicon-based liquid. In the summer of 1980, a switch was made to a glycol-based coolant, and seal-less magnetic drive pumps were installed. The problem was solved.

In designing an active solar installation, keep the mechanicals simple, Grover said. It should operate like a conventional system. Otherwise, when operators are not familiar with complex equipment, minor problems could lead to a difficult situation. "Design a system with little maintenance," Grover suggested.

Funded by the state of Connecticut and the federal National Guard, the total project (for both buildings) cost about $1,459,000 or $36 per square foot. That cost included the active solar heating system at $2.19 per square foot ($88,490 total) and other energy saving components such as extra insulation and insulated windows for $1.35 per square foot ($54,600 total).

Built by F. W. Brown Construction Company of Yantic, Connecticut, the building also included energy saving features such as:

- Thermal walls with polystyrene foam panels sandwiched between a brick veneer exterior and concrete blocks;
- Windows on the south side of the building for winter heat gain;
- Woods on the northern exposure to provide a windbreak;
- A simplified solar system to save on construction costs. A costly roof supporting system could have doubled the cost of the solar system. The armory's solar system was designed to eliminate an unneeded storage tank.

In addition to these savings, ventilation was reduced in areas when unoccupied. All windows contain insulated glass. For cloudy, sunless days, an oil-fired hot air furnace and boiler provides backup heat.

A computer was used to simulate weather conditions, siting, square footage, materials, and occupancy to estimate the buildings' energy efficiency in the planning stages. Cost savings were estimated to pay back the initial investment in about twelve years.

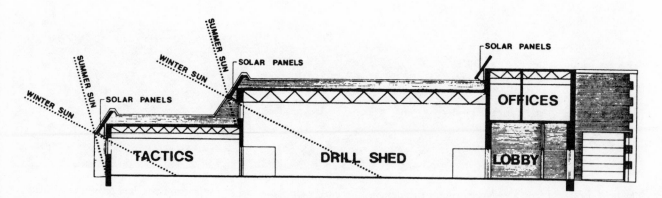

The cross-sectional drawing shows how winter heat gain is maximized through south-facing windows. The active solar panels act as overhangs to shade the glass areas from the hot summer sun.

Passive Solar Adds a Custom Touch

Even in the late 1970s, it was easy to spot a solar house. They looked different. They were easily identified as "solar." But now, "we are in the third generation of passive solar design," said Atlanta architect Bill Witte of Thompson, Hancock, Witte & Associates. "Designs are now much more acceptable in the marketplace." And although he feels that people expressed more anxiety over energy costs in previous years, they are now much more interested in passive solar, due to improved designs.

To kick off a new custom development in Atlanta, Witte designed a passive solar model house in cooperation with the Southern Solar Energy Center (a regional office of the Department of Energy), custom builder Jim Brown of Roswell, Georgia, and the developer of Chimney Lakes, Arvida Realty Sales. "Our key goal was to design a reasonable, readily acceptable, marketable passive solar house that could be incorporated into any development," Witte said. "It is highly marketable from interior and exterior aesthetics to the functional floor plan."

Most people who are not familiar with passive solar energy look for something unusual, said builder Jim Brown. Visitors to the passive solar model "expected to find Star Wars technology." Most were pleasantly surprised by what they found.

The 2329-square-foot, demonstration house was completed and opened to visitors in conjunction with the grand opening of the Chimney Lakes development in October 1980. During four weeks of an open house, about seventy-seven hundred people visited the model. The model house was sold prior to the opening for $134,000, including upgrades and a $20,000 lot. Brown estimated that a similar passive solar house could be constructed without the upgrades for about $120,000.

For the opening, the unit was furnished and decorated to help show off the passive solar features and broaden its appeal to the public. "We felt that the passive solar aspect would not be as successfully merchandised without the furnishings or window treatments," said Harry Hammond, vice president of Arvida Realty Sales in Roswell, Georgia, and division director of sales and marketing. "The

model also showed that passive solar is practical and not outlandish. The house is a statement that energy conservation can be aesthetically pleasing."

Passive solar was not just an added feature in the house, architect Witte said. It was an integral aspect. The plan was designed so that the most-used areas of the house—the family room, kitchen and dining room—could take maximum advantage of natural daylight.

One of the most appealing rooms in the house was an enclosed sun porch or Florida room. Incorporating passive solar techniques, it also was designed to be used about 80 percent of the year, providing additional living and entertaining space, natural light and views to interior spaces, and a greenhouse for plants.

Brown conservatively estimated that the house will save about 15 percent on heating costs. A computer analysis estimated 40 to 60 percent savings. But as Brown pointed out, savings depend on the energy efficiency of the comparable unit. Actual savings will be monitored.

The passive solar system added about $2500 to the cost of the model house, including extra ductwork, water storage drums and a glass wall in the basement, and thermal storage rods. The rods, located in the sun space on the back wall of the master bedroom, contain a salt-water solution that absorbs heat and gradually releases the heat when the temperature falls below 81 degrees Fahrenheit. Vents located above the rods distribute the heat into the great room. Vents in the dining room enable the air to be recirculated through the storage system in the basement. The windows in the master bedroom can also be opened to allow heat to flow into other living areas of the house.

The added cost of the passive solar system did not include double-glazed thermal pane glass used throughout the house, R19 wall insulation, and R30 ceiling insulation. Every glazed area has an overhang or trellis to prevent summer heat gain, Witte said.

From a marketing approach, the house provided a livable plan with living areas located at the rear of the unit. Functional space, aesthetics, and energy conservation were all important considerations in the plan and design of the house, Hammond said.

Passive solar energy savings were incorporated into the design of a demonstration home which kicked off the grand opening of Chimney Lakes, a custom development near Atlanta.

A sun room (shown at right) acted as a passive solar heat "collector" but it also served as additional living and entertaining space and as a source of natural light for interior living spaces.

SECOND FLOOR

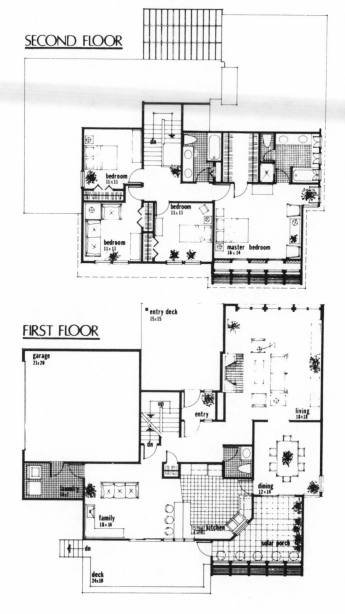

bedroom
11×11

bedroom
11×11

bedroom
11×11

master bedroom
16×14

FIRST FLOOR

entry deck
15×15

garage
21×20

up

entry

living
18×18

dn

dn

dining
12×14

family
18×14

kitchen

solar porch

deck
24×30

The family room, kitchen, and dining room were oriented to the south to maximize the benefits of passive solar heat and light in the most-used areas of the house. A portion of the solar porch extended to the second floor to provide passive solar heat to the master bedroom area. The plans were designed by architect Bill Witte of Thompson, Hancock, Witte & Associates.

Passive Solar Energy Features for Natural Heating and Cooling

Water wall for solar heating and storage;
Two-story sunspace for heating and heat distribution;
Wide overhangs;
Special trellis for seasonal heating control;
Masonry floors to store solar heat;
Circulation system to distribute heated air from the sunspace and water wall;
Site orientation;
Insulation;
Tight shell construction for infiltration control;
Vestibule to serve as an air-lock;
Less-used spaces located along northern exposure;
Garage on northwest side to protect living areas from winter wind;
Landscaping for a winter wind break and summer shade;
Wood frame and double-glazed windows.

SOURCE: Southern Solar Energy Center.

Add a Sun Spa for Passive Solar Heat

Active solar systems were great for collecting and storing heat, but it was soon recognized that they were not the only way to harness the sun. Passive solar design, it was found, could collect solar heat without sophisticated equipment. Both builders and architects agreed that passive solar design could be an important energy saving feature in any house, conventional or active solar.

One Seattle architect looked on the bright side of passive solar design, by including a sun spa on a basic, 1900-square-foot home. The solarium resulted in added living space, solar heat gain, natural ventilation, and lighting. The space is basically added to the rear, south-facing elevation of the house, a technique which could be adapted for new construction and remodeling.

Architect Omer Mithun designed the house specifically to return the most energy savings for the least investment on an average-size, two-story, single-family, detached house. The house was commissioned by the American Plywood Association and Family Circle magazine. It was completed in the fall of 1977.

The solarium combined a number of passive energy savers while enhancing the design of the house and adding valuable living space.

Habitable for most of the year, the solarium faces south to absorb the winter sun like a greenhouse. The solarium is basically a patio enclosed with single-glazed glass and sliding glass doors for ventilation. Although it looks like an energy waster, the solarium actually saves energy by acting as an insulating air-jacket between the house and the outdoors. The jacket saves energy by helping reduce heat loss. But the solarium also produces its own heat. It is not conventionally heated. The sun warms the solarium and the rest of the house during the day. (See photo on page 71.)

A tile floor in the solarium retains heat to help keep the air warm at night. To supplement solar heat gain, a conventional heat pump acts as a backup source of heat. The solarium design is adaptable for other regions of the country, particularly in northern climates, said architect Mithun.

The 432-square-foot solarium is accessible through sliding glass doors in the living, dining, and kitchen areas. Built-in cabinets and a wet bar make the room into an extended family or living area. Windows in the second story bedrooms overlook the solarium for natural light, heat, and ventilation.

But to prevent overheating, the upper floor was extended four feet over the lower living level to shade against summer sun. Sliding glass doors in the solarium open to the outside for ventilation and natural cooling in summer. Also, hot air at the top of the solarium can be vented into the attic where it is pulled outside.

In addition, shades on the solarium windows pull down for summer shading or heat retention on winter nights.

Constructed by the Swanson-Dean Corp. of Bellevue, Washington, the two-bedroom house with den was designed to be adaptable to most code and climatic areas of the country, with minor modifications. Sun angles, the overhang, and insu-

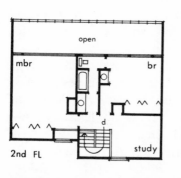

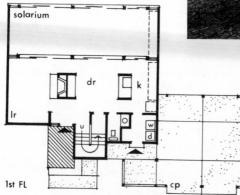

The solarium consisted of 432 square feet on the south side of the house. Constructed in Seattle, Washington, in 1977 for about $31 per square foot, the 1900-square-foot house was designed to absorb solar heat "without moving parts." Interior photos show how screens and the upper floor help shade the house from the hot summer sun. The plans were designed by Omer Mithun. PHOTOS: American Plywood Association.

lation requirements may differ according to the latitude and heating needs.

The house sold in 1977 for about $55,000 to $60,000, excluding land. Construction costs were about $31 per square foot.

A Design for Saving Energy . . .
and the Environment

Energy savings is not always a choice, sometimes it is a necessity. In remote areas, the use of passive and active solar systems can help provide a significant contribution when energy sources are unavailable, scarce, or expensive.

When the National Audubon Society wanted to build a visitor center in a South Carolina swamp, they wanted more than a building. They wanted to express a concern for the natural environment. Located in the 3500-acre Four Holes Swamp in the Francis Beidler Forest, thirty-five miles northwest of Charleston, South Carolina, the building was constructed on poles to aid natural growth and water run-off and not disturb tree root systems. The building was constructed about five feet above the ground with poles extending through the building itself.

The structure was located on dry land adjacent to the swamp area. But the inaccessibility of the site and concern for the natural wildlife and vegetation posed construction problems. Building materials had to be delivered while preserving natural vegetation. Construction workers were on the constant lookout for wildlife such as insects, snakes, alligators, and water moccasins.

The National Audubon Society's visitors' center was built on the edge of a swamp to act as an educational display on the ecology of the area. The boardwalk (shown) extended through the swamp and heavy natural growth. Passive solar design and active solar collectors were designed to provide about 67 percent of the heating and hot water needs.

The remote site also meant that the only available source of heat was electricity. To help reduce the cost of conditioning the center for an estimated thirty-thousand visitors year-round, the 2400-square-foot center was designed to be energy responsive as well as environmentally sensitive.

The mechanical system itself was designed to express an ecological message to visitors. Architect Walter Pate designed the building with passive and active solar systems incorporated into the structure. Completed in 1978, construction costs reached $78,225, excluding the cost of the active solar system, site development, and the parking lot.

First, passive solar design techniques were incorporated to reduce heat gain in summer and heat loss in winter. Heavily insulated walls, floors, and ceilings were a start. The amount of north- and west-facing glass was reduced. South-facing glass was designed specifically to maximize use of the winter sun and to shade out summer sun—an important consideration in summer climates. The collection of solar heat gain through south-facing windows was estimated to provide about 51 percent of the heating requirements of the building on a sunny mid-winter day. Hot air which rose to the top of the clerestory ceiling was redistributed by a

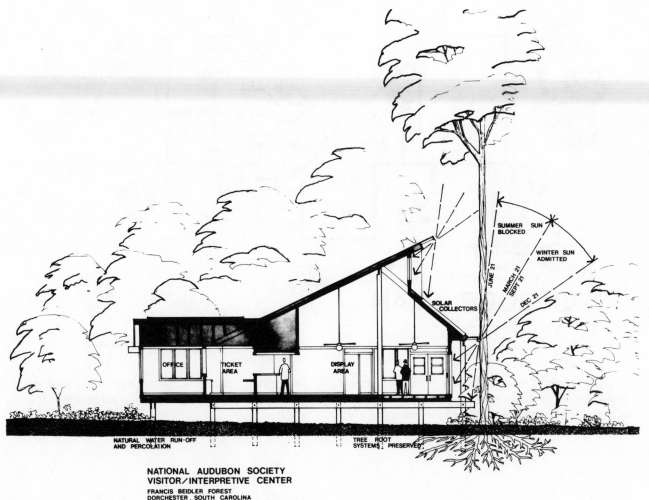

NATIONAL AUDUBON SOCIETY
VISITOR/INTERPRETIVE CENTER
FRANCIS BEIDLER FOREST
DORCHESTER, SOUTH CAROLINA
WALTER F. PATE, AIA ARCHITECT

The overhang on the south end of the building blocked out the summer sun while allowing passive solar heat gain during winter months. The location of the solar collectors is also shown.

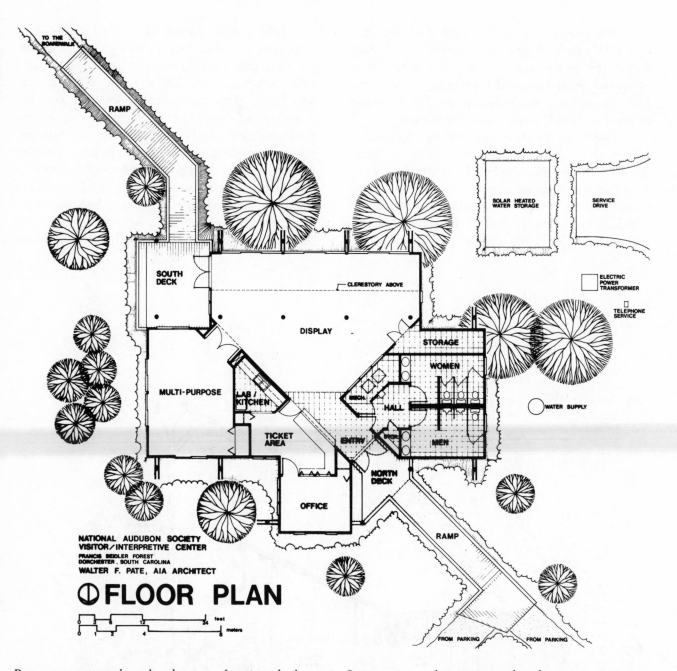

FLOOR PLAN

NATIONAL AUDUBON SOCIETY
VISITOR/INTERPRETIVE CENTER
FRANCIS BEIDLER FOREST
DORCHESTER, SOUTH CAROLINA
WALTER F. PATE, AIA ARCHITECT

Rooms were arranged to take advantage of passive solar heat gain. Service areas, such as storage and washrooms, were not cooled in summer and only minimally heated in winter. And when not in use, the multi-purpose room could be closed off to save energy. The plans were designed by architect Walter Pate.

duct to the heating system in the winter (and exhausted from the building in the summer).

Room arrangements also took passive solar ideas in mind. Rooms that were not regularly occupied, such as storage, mechanical, and rest rooms, were not cooled in summer and only minimally heated in winter. Also, the multipurpose room could be closed off when not in use.

The second part of the solar heating system included active solar collection. The 360 square feet of collectors were estimated to provide about 74 percent of the heating requirements of the building on a sunny mid-winter day. Combined with the passive solar heat gain, an estimated 23 percent of excess heat from the active system was stored in a 4000-gallon tank for later use during cloudy or rainy weather. Solar was designed to provide about 67 percent of the heating requirements of the building with an additional 33 percent supplied from backup sources.

A water source heat pump utilized the heat stored in the water tanks when the active and passive solar systems could not supply enough heat for the building. Also, when there was not a sufficient amount of heat in the storage tanks and the outside temperature rose above 40 degrees Fahrenheit, an air source heat pump was used to supply heat.

Electric resistance heat was the only available backup system for the remote location. Based on an average heating season of four months at four cents per kilowatt hour, the total annual heating cost of a comparable conventional building would be about $900 to $1000, or about $225 per month during the winter.

But with the incorporation of the passive and active solar systems and solar-assisted heat pump, the energy costs for the building were estimated at about $150 to $200 per heating season, or about $38 to $50 per month during the winter.

But in South Carolina, cooling needs were also a serious consideration. For passive solar design, roof overhangs and retention of natural vegetation were incorporated to help shade glazed areas in summer months. Natural ventilation was aided by ceiling fans, sliding glass doors, and the clerestory roof design. The same heat pump was designed also to cool the building by storing cold water in the same 4000-gallon solar storage tank during off-peak hours, to help keep down energy costs. Because of the reduced load, a three-ton rather than a five-ton compressor was used. Also, to help reduce the need for electricity, the building was designed to take advantage of natural light from view windows and the clerestory windows.

Design and energy efficiency are important parts of any solar house. But from a builder's perspective, marketability is also a vital element. Solar was marketed successfully in this townhouse development in Boulder, Colorado.

4

MARKETING THE SOLAR HOUSE

Through hands-on experience, builders learned that they can build solar homes. They learned how the systems perform, how to install them, and what are the best construction techniques to employ.

Solar works on the construction site. Builders have proved it. But that is only one-half of the learning process. Builders also need to know: Does it work in the marketplace? Does solar sell? The builder wears two hats. He is also a salesperson.

Solar is an attractive and valuable energy-saving feature. But just as it should not dominate the architecture of the house, solar should not be the sole focus of the marketing program. Energy efficiency is a significant factor in the home buying decision. But it is not the only one.

Builders have learned through actual experience that while energy savings are important to buyers, advertising a home as solar does not guarantee its sale. Selling a solar home is basically no different from selling a conventional home. Solar does not automatically put a marketing edge on a home. Much more is involved. Solar is merely an investment in energy savings which will increase in value over the years as conventional energy prices escalate. Solar should be marketed as such, not as the most dominant feature of the house.

Buyers are seeking energy efficiency in the homes they buy and taking serious second looks at the potential of solar energy in making homes even more energy efficient. Solar heat or water heating is an important and effective energy-saving feature,

according to 30 percent of prospective home buyers in a 1980 *Professional Builder* survey. About 28 percent also thought that solar water heating was a good investment and that they were willing to purchase a system in the new home they buy. Some 58 percent were a bit more skeptical and said that they would prefer to wait a few years before investing in a solar water-heating system.

But attitudes towards solar energy are often shaped by its unavailability on the marketplace. Of those in the survey who said that they would not purchase a solar system, over 40 percent indicated that solar was not available in their area. Of those who did not consider a solar energy system a good investment, about 28 percent admitted that they just did not know why—indicating that consumers need good reliable information from builders about solar homes.

The lack of information about solar energy was one of the reasons the HUD solar demonstration program was conducted: to let the public learn about solar by visiting (and purchasing) actual solar homes in the marketplace. The market impact of the demonstration program was significant. In the period of 1975 to 1979, HUD awarded 783 grants to support demonstrations of solar heating, cooling, and water-heating systems in 12,423 dwellings across the United States.

In general, for those who purchased the solar homes built with the HUD grants, solar was not the major motivating factor in their decisions first to visit the home and then to buy it. Most listed the location of the house, its price, size, and style as the primary reasons for buying the solar residence. Fewer than 10 percent said that the solar system was the most important factor in their decision to buy, according to a HUD report. Almost all of the builders indicated that a solar demonstration home definitely increased traffic through the models or subdivision, but fewer than one-half believed that the solar unit boosted sales of other models in the subdivision.

Buyer response to the solar homes built under the demonstration program varied widely. One builder in Ohio said that he offered a solar option in his other models, "but there were no takers. Regular fuels are not too expensive yet," he said. Another builder said that his customers in Georgia balked at the additional cost of active solar equipment. High initial costs were the barrier. "Few are willing to invest, but all are interested," a Minnesota builder said. His sentiment was echoed in 1979 by a builder in Florida: "Buyers are stretching to be able to afford the housing unit. If solar is added to the price, they might not qualify for the mortgage." But it should be noted that tax credits and more careful consideration of monthly utility costs in the qualification of buyers by lenders are helping to diminish the impact of high initial costs.

Many builders in the demonstration program indicated that while the solar houses drew crowds of sightseers, few serious buyers were in the bunch. In Colorado, one advertisement in the newspaper drew one hundred and seventy-five people to see the house. But the house stood four months unsold on the market. Other builders had similar problems. "The customer has a fear of the unknown," said a New York builder. About eight thousand people toured his house, "but no one wanted to buy it." Many indicated that solar was an impediment in selling the house.

But in many cases, solar became a scapegoat for why the solar house did not sell immediately. Some sales resistance may *not* have been attributable to the solar system, but to the house itself or to the way it was marketed. One builder in Oklahoma was unable to sell his first solar house, "not solely due to the solar heating system, but rather to the

house design," he said. His second solar home was designed with a more conventional appearance and was "better accepted by the people in the area."

State and federal tax credits or tax deductions have been helpful to many in marketing and selling some solar homes. But initially many builders said that the tax breaks were "only a gimmick," "insufficient," "confusing," or "not great enough to overcome resistance." One builder in Indiana observed in 1979 that while a tax credit exists in his state, "even the state auditors don't know how to apply it." Builders had trouble explaining the tax breaks to buyers because they did not understand the legislation themselves. But since then, tax credits available for the installation of some types of solar systems have been used by many builders effectively as a marketing tool to help turn prospects into actual buyers.

Builder experience in the demonstration program had increasing impact as builders fine-tuned the construction process, established their reputations and experience in building solar, and as buyers realized actual savings. One North Carolina builder noted that when he sold his solar houses in 1978, his buyers were mostly indifferent to the solar systems. Prospective buyers were curious and considered the solar a novelty. But since then, he noticed a change in attitudes. One of his four "ho-hum" buyers wrote him a letter stating that he was "very glad that he had the solar system." And among his prospective buyers, many serious inquiries about solar homes have emerged.

But despite reports of marketing problems, other builders in the HUD program reported positive marketing experiences with their initial solar houses and the sale of subsequent ones. "The solar house was sold the third day that it was open," said a builder in Utah. One Indiana builder said that 75 percent of the people interested in purchasing his homes ask if the solar system can be added to their new homes later on.

Builders said that publicity about initial problems in early solar houses and the lack of public education about solar were major sales barriers in the late 1970s. But those misconceptions and barriers began diminishing as solar houses became more common in market areas.

Builders also learned that emphasis on payback periods may discourage prospective buyers. Long payback periods of many initial active solar systems tended to scare away buyers, particularly in highly mobile areas. One builder in Texas indicated that his retired customers "felt that they will not live long enough to gain a payback." In his case, a marketing program emphasizing lower monthly utility bills for those on fixed incomes would have promoted the positive advantages of the solar system.

Prospective buyers were also sometimes skeptical about the future of solar technology. Many felt that solar was still in its developmental stage and was likely to change considerably in the coming years as a result of advancements in technology. "They're afraid that today's product will be out-of-date in five years," said a Virginia builder. But many builders responded by indicating to their buyers that in coming years a non-solar house may prove to be obsolete in comparison with a conventional energy-guzzler.

Builders have noticed that experience with solar helps considerably with buyers. As builders gain experience and feel more comfortable with solar construction and marketing, a feeling of confidence is passed onto the buyer, thereby creating more positive attitudes about solar. Marketing lessons were as important to early solar builders as the construction experience. Based on their track records, other builders have been able to develop successful merchandising programs for solar homes.

The HUD demonstration program produced substantial amounts of information on how solar works in the marketplace. "The most positive response (towards solar demonstration homes) has been experienced by builders who have provided information about how their systems work and who have not made unrealistic predictions about expected fuel savings," one HUD report stated.

A sales staff trained in merchandising solar homes is a necessity in providing accurate and marketable information to prospective buyers. Builders should make sure that the sales staff or realtors understand how the basic system operates and what realistic—not overstated—savings are to be expected from the solar system. Brochures, general

literature about solar, and third-party documentation can aid the sales effort. Many builders include the solar system among a list of other energy-saving features in their model home brochures. That way, energy efficiency is promoted without undue emphasis on the solar system. Third-party documentation, such as estimated energy savings from utility companies, actual heating bills, and monitored savings provides good credibility in the minds of prospective home buyers.

Builders should not assume that buyers understand what solar is all about. In determining the effects of solar in the home-buying decision, the Solar Energy Research Institute conducted a study in 1981 of over two thousand randomly selected homeowners and about four thousand actual solar homeowners. About 73 percent of the non-solar respondents said that they did not know enough about solar energy to make a decision about using it in their homes. Only about 25 percent said that they felt they knew enough to decide.

Information is the key in reaching and broadening the appeal of solar in the market. It can help erase the hesitancy to try "something new." Careful training of sales staff, explanatory brochures, sales center displays, and third-party documentation all can help in merchandising the solar home.

One report from HUD cautioned builders against designing the merchandising program primarily around the solar features. Too much attention to the solar aspects of the house can be harmful. "Advertising campaigns which emphasize solar and nothing else may draw lots of people . . . but they don't generally attract any more serious buyers than standard promotions," the report noted. "And in one case, the circus-like atmosphere that was created was a deterrent: As the house became an object of curiosity, it ceased to be thought of as a place to live. . . . Good marketing plans for solar homes have differed very little from the conventional methods of marketing conventional homes," it was concluded.

Any builder who knows his or her market can sell solar as well. The merchandising of solar housing must be geared towards the buyer, from the style and design of the house to the location, price, and other amenities. Particularly for the economy-minded buyer, lower monthly utility costs can turn solar into a marketing plus, if merchandised properly. Extra care should be made in keeping estimated savings realistic and not overrated. A lower estimate pleases homeowners when their actual savings exceed the estimates. But inflated estimates of energy savings can produce dissatisfaction, no matter how much the house actually may have saved.

It is also recommended that in most solar houses, builders emphasize solar's short-term monthly savings rather than the system's long-term payback period. The buyer will see results of the solar system in the first month of occupancy in the form of lower fuel bills. But a long-term payback period can produce a deterrent in the buyer's mind. Although the system will eventually pay for itself, few buyers may expect to live in the house for that length of time. And often a calculated payback period is based solely on energy savings. Federal and state tax credits can make a significant difference in the "real" cost of the solar system to the buyer.

Increased home resale value also can be used as a strong marketing angle in solar sales. As the cost of heating and cooling a home with conventional fuels continues to escalate, the solar home becomes even more valuable to the owner—in monthly savings *and* in the resale market among other buyers.

Buyer satisfaction is also an important marketing tool. Satisfaction among solar homeowners means positive word-of-mouth advertising for the builder and a positive image for solar. It has been noted that as builders gain experience in constructing marketable solar homes, positive reaction to solar home ownership has increased markedly. A HUD study published in mid-1980 by the Real Estate Research Corporation included the results of interviews with 132 buyers of active solar homes constructed under the HUD solar demonstration program. Of the home buyers, 58 percent were initially satisfied with their solar homes. Six months later, over 90 percent expressed satisfaction with the house and 75 percent said that they would consider buying a solar house again.

Other studies among solar homeowners also show that an overwhelming majority are satisfied with their solar-energy systems. Six independent research studies of more than one thousand owners of solar systems conducted between 1977 and 1979 showed that 82 percent to 93 percent of owners were either "satisfied" or "very satisfied." In four of the studies, surveying a total of 877 owners, more than 90 percent of the respondents reported satisfaction with their solar systems.

Most of the information collected on the attitudes of home buyers towards solar and about the marketing potential of solar homes has been derived from surveys and interviews with those who actually bought solar houses. These polls contain valuable lessons on the marketing of solar homes. But buyer information is supplemented and supported by builder experience.

Merchandising programs for solar homes will vary across the country, dependent on the local housing markets. But over and over, it has been noted that many builders in the early stages of solar development focused entirely too much attention on the solar system, ignoring the basics of merchandising homes. A buyer purchases a home for more reasons than the type of heating system it contains. But builders learned that solar does provide a positive influence on the buying decision as an energy-saving amenity. Solar *can* provide a marketing edge over other homes in the area, but only if all other factors are equal. Solar could, therefore, swing the sale. But it will not necessarily make the sale. There is a big difference.

Because it will not sell strictly on the merits of utilizing solar energy, many builders have underplayed a house's solar aspects in advertising campaigns. Whereas solar or energy efficiency may be listed among the project's amenities, solar should not be the sole calling card for the development, in most cases.

Solar can be used as a strong marketing tool. But the basics of good merchandising apply to those with solar features just as they apply to those without. A lemon with a solar system is still a lemon. A HUD report pointed out, "the deciding factor in the sale and purchase of the solar house is rarely the solar energy system alone. It is the right combination of the house, amenities, location, prospective buyer, and price."

HUD Demo Program: The First Step for Solar Construction

Solar grants awarded through the residential solar demonstration program in the mid-1970s funded through the Department of Housing and Urban Development were instrumental in getting solar off the ground. Thanks to financial influence of the four-year, five-cycle federal subsidy plan, thousands of solar houses and apartments were constructed across the country. Builders who constructed solar houses as a result of the subsidy program reported heavy traffic of house hunters through the solar units.

Wonderland Hills, a planned unit development in Boulder, Colorado, was one example. The opening of a solar-powered townhouse in 1977 brought out big crowds and resulted in a sell-out of thirty-five HUD-subsidized, solar townhomes in two weeks. Wonderland Hills Development Co. officials believed that if a large number of solar units could be constructed on a demonstration basis, momentum could be generated to sell other solar sections in their development.

General manager Jim Leach said that the HUD grant of $146,000 for thirty-five townhome units added credibility to Wonderland Hills' earlier solar program. The company had offered a solar option for heating and hot water on its homes and had built a solar townhome on speculation. But Leach said that the grant gave them a tremendous boost, enough to "put us in the business."

Part of the design concept was to keep the solar units from looking different from the rest of the community. Solar and non-solar townhomes were constructed in the same style with the same materials. Both have the same roof pitch as well. At a 5–12 pitch, the roofs were not considered optimal for solar and the collectors would lose about 8 percent efficiency. But this compromise permitted solar to be included in non-solar communities without disrupting the overall look.

Wonderland Hills' first attempt at solar was on the end unit of a three-unit townhouse configuration, built without aid of a federal grant (end unit shown). Including a solar system worth about $8,500, the solar townhome unit sold in 1977 for about $95,000 with no subsidy.

At the same time that they were beginning to construct the HUD units, Wonderland Hills held a public open house in the existing solar unit. In a two-week period and amidst a crowd of home buyers, engineers, curiosity seekers, and students,

The land plan shows the siting of the seven 5-unit town-homes constructed in Wonderland Hills, Boulder, Colorado and funded through the HUD residential solar demonstration program in 1977.

Solar collectors shown on the townhouse help provide heat and hot water for the end unit. Built on speculation, the design demonstrated that solar systems could be added without changing the overall look of the development.

all thirty-five units were reserved with $500 down-payments. In the framing stages, firm contracts were drawn up, selling the units for $46,000 to $65,000 (see photo on page 107).

With the HUD grant, a one-third cost saving on the solar system was passed on to the buyer. The grant provided about $4,200 per unit, but the solar system cost between $5,000 and $8,000 per unit to install. The cost for the average solar system consisted of:

Solar hardware, panels and air handler	$3250
Heat storage	500
Sheet metal and installation labor	1000
Engineering, overhead, and supervision	500
Sales and finance costs	500
Builder's profit	250
Total Sales Price	$6000

HUD was available for technical advice, but Leach said that they did not need much help. With the aid of a Solaron Corporation training seminar, the heating subcontractor and some of the crew learned the nuts and bolts of solar construction and operation.

Using Solaron air-type collectors, the system was designed to attain about 50 percent of the unit's energy needs. In actual operation of the first unit, occupants received better results. A forced-air, electric furnace and conventional electric water heater were included as a backup system.

Leach said that the solar system was just part of the total energy-saving package. Additional energy savers in the townhomes included: 6-inch side walls and studs at 24 inches on center to allow for more insulation; 12 inches blown R30 attic insulation; ¾-inch extruded polystyrene foam sheathing giving the walls an R22 insulative value; double-

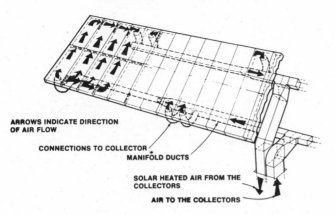

TYPICAL COLLECTOR INSTALLATION

ARROWS INDICATE DIRECTION
OF AIR FLOW

CONNECTIONS TO COLLECTOR
MANIFOLD DUCTS

SOLAR HEATED AIR FROM THE
COLLECTORS

AIR TO THE COLLECTORS

In an air-type solar system, air flows from the inlet duct through the collector panels where it is heated, down to the end of the row and to ducting in the attic. Insulated ducts take the solar heated air to the basement for storage or direct heating. Diagram courtesy of the Solaron Corporation.

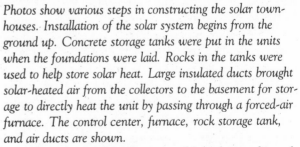

Photos show various steps in constructing the solar townhouses. Installation of the solar system begins from the ground up. Concrete storage tanks were put in the units when the foundations were laid. Rocks in the tanks were used to help store solar heat. Large insulated ducts brought solar-heated air from the collectors to the basement for storage to directly heat the unit by passing through a forced-air furnace. The control center, furnace, rock storage tank, and air ducts are shown.

The crew fits the collector panels together on the roof of one of the 5-unit townhomes built through the HUD program. It is shown in the final construction stages.

glazed windows with a plastic thermal break; recirculating vent fans; fan-forced air fireplace; and an attic vent fan.

Documenting Buyer Satisfaction with Solar

Many builders use energy efficiency and solar features as merchandising tools. But few know how these features actually affected the purchase decision of their home buyers.

In June 1979, builder Jim Gregory of The Gregory Company in Irvine, California, completed his Seabluff Canyon townhome project in Costa Mesa, California. The eighty-two units included passive solar design concepts and active solar-assisted water heating as standard features. The 1234-square-foot to 1761-square-foot townhomes were priced in 1979 from the high $70,000s to the mid $90,000s.

To determine the effect of the solar features on the homeowners' purchase decisions, Gregory interviewed his homeowners six months later in December 1979. As a result of the study, it was determined that solar was not a key influence on the purchase decision. But after only six months of living in the units, 94 percent of the homeowners were pleased with the results of the solar features. "Most didn't buy because of the solar," said Gregory. "It was not until afterwards that solar became a more important ingredient."

The report noted that most purchase decisions are based on a variety of factors, rather than a single attribute, and on the ability of the home to fulfill a range of needs. A report on the survey was prepared for the Gregory Company by Steven L. Roth in April 1980.

Survey results illustrated the buyers' initial and subsequent reaction to the inclusion of solar features in their homes. On their first visit to the project, 28 percent of the homeowners said that they were impressed with the solar and energy-conserving features. Six months later, 34 percent said that they were now more impressed with these features than on their initial visit. About 15 percent said that the solar features actually influenced their purchase decision.

In the survey, not one homeowner indicated anxiety about the solar components. Among the 82 units, only one system required one service call—to Gregory's surprise and relief. System malfunctions were one of his initial apprehensions about including solar in the project at all. He attributed the lack of service problems to a reliable and conscientious contractor who continued to follow up and check on the systems even after installation. He considered the use of a good solar contractor as an important element in the success of any solar project.

The active and passive solar features included: active solar collectors to supply an estimated 80 percent of the homes' hot water needs; atriums and skylights for natural heat and lighting; shading for windows and doors; water-saving devices; well-insulated exterior walls and ceilings; and pilotless equipment for space heating.

The passive solar benefits and active solar-assisted water heating were not emphasized in the brochure. They were only listed as "hidden values." But about 72 percent of the homeowners stated that they were aware of the passive solar features and 64 percent were able to identify Grumman Sunstream as the manufacturer of the solar water heating system, indicating good informational techniques by the sales staff.

In the six-month study, 72 percent of the homeowners recommended that solar and energy-conserving features should be stressed in an advertising campaign, indicating their potential strength as marketing tools in the eyes of buyers.

The actual utility bills also increased the significance of solar among the homeowners. Residents said that in their previous dwellings, their gas bills averaged about $12.81, compared with $7.87 in the solar residence. Yet, 66 percent of the homeowners also pointed out that their previous residences were smaller in square footage.

After six months of living in the solar townhomes, 46 percent of the homeowners said that they justified the $2500 expenditure for the solar-assisted water heater. Savings on utility bills were one reason. Also, buyers were able to claim a federal tax credit of 40 percent on the initial cost of the system. The California state tax credit of 55 percent was taken by the builder to help offset costs.

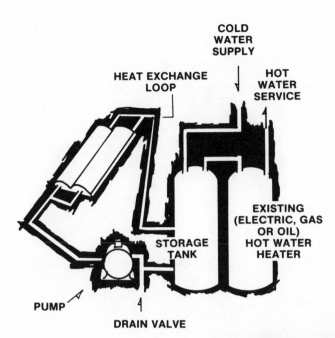

COLD WATER SUPPLY

HEAT EXCHANGE LOOP

HOT WATER SERVICE

EXISTING (ELECTRIC, GAS OR OIL) HOT WATER HEATER

STORAGE TANK

PUMP

DRAIN VALVE

Solar water heating and some passive solar design features were included in the Seabluff Canyon townhomes in Costa Mesa, California. Varied roof angles (as shown on the next page) allowed each unit access to the sun. The active solar water-heating system was used basically to preheat the water for domestic uses.

WHERE IS THE SUN?

Introducing homes of the future for foresighted homebuyers, Seabluff Canyon Townhomes in Costa Mesa employ the sun's free energy on a daily basis. The planned, ocean-view residential community is a development of The Gregory Company of Costa Mesa.

Sounds like science fiction, but the handsome two- and three-bedroom townhomes are constructed — through use of a solar-assisted domestic hot water heating system and passive solar floorplan designs — to save 50% of the energy costs required by currently available homes, at conservative estimate.

Deceptively traditional in appearance, using the rough cedar exteriors that weather so charmingly in seaside environments, the multi-level residences, priced in the range from the high $70,000's to the mid $90,000's, are plotted to steal every possible fraction of the sun's free energy and put it to work. And what cannot be captured by design is harnessed by technological expertise.

It turns out that energy-saving offers an exciting fringe benefit. Design elements arranged to ensnare heat and light through cross-ventilation, windows and sun-and-star filled skylights also achieve effects of dramatic beauty.

Grumman Sunstream was selected to provide the special system which uses the sun's free energy to preheat water, and in turn reduce conventional energy requirements for heating the water to necessary temperatures for home use. Further energy savers include heavy insulation, double-glazed glass at especially sunny or shady windows, water-saving devices, and pilotless equipment wherever possible. And wood-burning fireplaces are not only decorative — they're energy-savers, too.

Just eighty-two innovative townhomes — with six floorplans containing from 1,234 to 1,762 square feet of interior living space and a lot more with spacious decks will be available. Appointments are luxurious, and kitchens gourmet-equipped.

Recreation facilities include a double-decker clubhouse with solarium, kitchen and conversation area, and a swimming pool, spa, and tennis court. Maybe a future windmill, to let ocean breezes help with electricity.

To step into your future at Seabluff Canyon Townhomes, drive to Sea Bluff Drive (formerly Hamilton Street) and Canyon Drive in Costa Mesa. Plan to relax and watch the sun work!

... IT'S WORKING OVERTIME AT SEABLUFF CANYON TOWNHOMES IN COSTA MESA

New Homes Magazine

117

Seabluff Canyon Townhomes

The study concluded that the solar features enabled prospective home buyers to differentiate the Seabluff Canyon townhomes from competing townhome projects. The energy-saving features, including the solar elements, helped make the townhomes stand out from the rest. From a marketing standpoint, that can be an important element in the success of a project.

Gregory evaluated that Seabluff Canyon was "a successful project with positive acceptance." In addition to the solar townhomes, Gregory completed an active and passive solar commercial office building in April 1980. Future plans for solar residential and commercial projects continued to be researched by his firm, most particularly utilizing centralized solar heating systems.

Solar Interest Indicated in Market Demand

Crowds at demonstration model houses indicate strong consumer interest in solar energy. But the real interest is indicated best in sales.

Spec builder John Whitcombe of Tandem Properties in Davis, California, says that he can't build solar houses fast enough. "I've got five buyers for every house," he said. He developed his own solar system about four years ago to provide solar heating, cooling, and hot water in his tract housing and apartments.

Other builders took note. And as a result of the strong interest in his system, he established a separate firm, Trident Energy Systems, to market the system to other builders.

In the past four years, he installed about two hundred solar systems in his own $55,000 to $85,000 single-family homes and in apartment projects. Through Trident, he sold seventy systems to other builders in 1980. In 1981, he expected to sell four hundred systems to other builders.

In 1975, he found that even though the market demanded innovative energy-saving techniques, there were no solar systems really designed for the tract builder. Sometimes it is easier to do it yourself. Whitcombe developed his own system to meet his market's needs and his own specifications.

"The basic criteria was to design a system that is cost effective," he said. He wanted a system that could be adapted to his own floorplans and installed by his own subcontractors. For efficiency, Whitcombe insisted that the system be automatic.

In the application of solar energy in residential structures, "there is a bottleneck at the builder level," he said. "Builders need a system that is easy to implement."

The result of Whitcombe's quest was the development of a hybrid system that incorporated passive solar techniques and active solar hardware. Based on four years of operation, the solar system in Davis, California, typically provided 70 percent of the heat and hot water on an annual basis. In a low humidity area like Davis, 100 percent of the cooling also was supplied. Polybutylene piping in the slab provides radiant heating and cooling. In winter, water is circulated through solar collectors during the day to provide heat. In summer, water is circulated through the solar collectors at night to provide natural cooling during the day. The water storage tank, backup water heater, and other mechanical equipment fit into a corner of the garage.

The system's computerized control box works similarly to a common thermostat. The display box, located on a hallway wall, indicates when the hot water tank is being heated by the collectors, when the floor tank water is being circulated through the collectors, and when the floor tank water is being circulated in the slab tubing. Another indicator light shows when the backup system is on. The homeowner is able to tell whether the solar system is working or not, just by looking at the control box.

The inside temperature is set by the homeowner, like a thermostat, and controlled automatically. When the temperature falls below a certain setting, the backup heating system automatically turns on. The control display also provides a digital read-out of the actual indoor temperature.

In addition to the slab piping, active solar hardware, and mechanical equipment, the houses are sited to take advantage of direct solar gain. But Whitcombe said that only about 5 to 10 percent of the heating is provided by passive solar gain. Other energy savers include slab-edge insulation, R11-insulated walls, and R30-insulated ceilings.

Tandem's solar houses ranged in 1980 from $55,000 to $85,000 including solar. The schematic drawing of the solar system shows how the basic system works. Water is circulated through the collectors and through polybutylene piping in the slab to provide radiant heating and cooling. A water heater provides a backup source of heat. The mechanical equipment fits into the corner of the garage (shown). The digital control box, located on an interior hallway wall, was designed to be set by the homeowner like a common thermostat. Indicator lights show when the solar or backup systems are working.

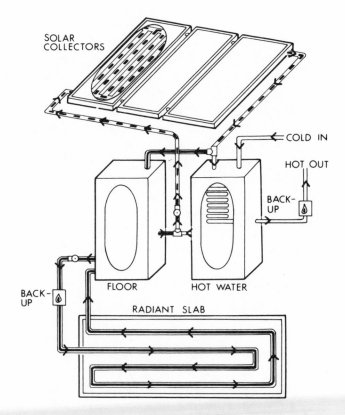

A solar apartment project was built by Tandem in 1980 for about $26 per square foot. Tandem's merchant houses were built in 1980 for about $32 to $35 per square foot, including solar.

Whitcombe admitted that in 1980 hard construction costs, the system was still not really cost effective. But federal and state tax credits made the system worth the extra initial cost.

The basic solar system for a 1500-square-foot house cost $7500 in 1980. But about $2500 was saved by not having to provide a conventional heating and cooling system. That brought the net additional cost down to $5000. And federal tax credits of $3000 made the incremental cost to the owner only $2000.

By adding $2000 to the mortgage of Tandem's typical house, approximately $22 is added to the monthly mortgage bill (at a 14 percent interest rate). But the energy savings make up more than the difference. In Davis, as a result of the solar system, owners saved between $30 and $40 per month on utility bills in 1980, Whitcombe said. In other areas of the country, he claimed that monthly savings would be even higher.

Whitcombe also pointed out that the cost of the solar system can be added on top of the mortgage ceiling established for loans insured by the Federal Housing Authority, resulting in a lower down payment for the home buyers.

Whitcombe is convinced that the consumer wants solar. Market demand—and sales—have proved it to him. "We have no fancy brochures or models," he said. "We don't need them. The solar system sells our houses."

Solar Sales: When It's Hot, It's Hot

Energy savings is not a buyer's prime consideration when buying a house, asserted builder Susan Barbash of Babylon, New York, but with location and product type being equal, buyers will opt for the energy-saving unit.

The solar water-heating option at the Sunscape townhomes in Bay Shore on Long Island, New York in August 1979 attracted the attention of the community and media. But it also attracted

sales. About 90 percent of the buyers at the project opted for the $2000 active solar water-heating system.

"They want to buy a good investment that will not become obsolete," Barbash noted. The monthly cost of the solar system and its monthly savings were displayed to buyers in the sales center (see charts below).

In the first three weekends of sales in August 1979, about 20 of the 79 units were sold. Buyers

ESTIMATED COST OF SOLAR SYSTEM

The solar system costs $2200, with a 20% down payment of $440 required. The down payment plus a one-time-only federal tax credit of $640 are figured into the first year's estimated cash savings of $211. Mortgage payments on the solar system average $187 per month.

	Solar Mortgage Payment	Electric Bill Reduction	Cumulative Cash Savings
First year	$187	$198	+211
Second year	187	218	+242
Third year	187	240	+295
Fourth year	187	264	+372
Fifth year	187	290	+475
Sixth year	187	319	+607
Seventh year	187	351	+771

PROJECTED ELECTRIC BILL SAVINGS

The Sunscape solar system should contribute 60% of the energy needed to heat 75 gallons of water per day at 140 degrees Fahrenheit. Electrical costs include 10% inflation rate escalator.

	Without Solar	With Solar
First year	$337	$129
Second year	371	142
Third year	408	156
Fourth year	448	171
Fifth year	493	188
Sixth year	542	207
Seventh year	597	228

The Sunscape townhome models in Bay Shore, New York, on Long Island, were designed for a conservative market and competitively priced. But they contained a big advantage: energy savings through conservation, passive and active solar heating.

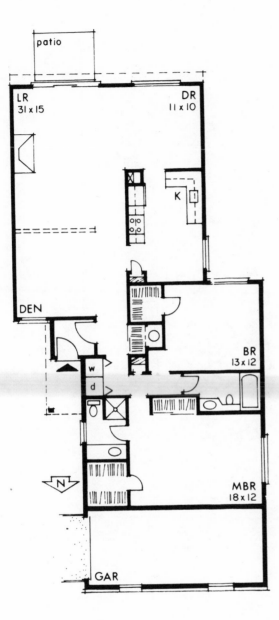

patio

LR
31 x 15

DR
11 x 10

K

DEN

BR
13 x 12

w

d

N

MBR
18 x 12

GAR

A floor plan of one of the Sunscape townhome models illustrates passive solar features built into the house designs. These include: glass and living areas on southern exposures for maximum passive solar heat gain; garage on north exposure to insulate the units from cold winter winds; and double-door entry vestibules to reduce heat loss.

percent of the buyers continue to purchase the solar option.

With her father Murray Barbash, a veteran Long Island builder, Susan Barbash decided to "go solar" *after* the initial plans for the townhome project had been already designed. Units were simply re-oriented towards the south with a few solar features added. "It was the easiest thing in the world to do," Barbash said, referring to the minor modifications. Even after the unit redesign, the larger units were simply transposed onto the same site plan without any necessary changes.

But the active solar water-heating option was only the beginning of the energy-saving features offered in the units. Passive solar features were incorporated into house design and siting.

Other standard energy-saving features included: R19-insulated exterior walls with six-inch studs, R30-insulated ceilings, double-glazed windows and patio doors, double-door entry vestibules, heating ducts placed within the building envelope to minimize heat loss, heat pumps, air returns in cathedral ceilings to redistribute stratified warm air in winter, water-saving faucets and fixtures, and two-foot overhangs on southern exposures for shading in summer months.

Estimated savings for space heat were expected to reach 21 percent to 43 percent, compared with 1979 New York State energy specifications. The projected savings were calculated by the local utility company and the heat pump manufacturer.

In actual operation, the estimated savings proved to be realistic. To calculate actual energy savings, utility bills for the solar units were compared with similar housing units in the area. In

were primarily local empty-nesters and young professional couples. The two- and three-bedroom units were priced from $72,990 to $85,990.

In April 1980, the units were redesigned to accommodate market demand in the area for larger, more luxurious housing, particularly for empty-nesters and affluent young professionals. The larger units ranged from 2200 to 2300 square feet from an attached ranch with two-car garage to a two-story townhome with a two-car garage. The redesigned units were priced from $105,000 to $113,000 with a $3,000 solar option. About 90

The Sunscape site plan shows how units were clustered to take advantage of a southern exposure. Views were oriented towards greenbelt areas and a man-made lake.

December 1980, considering an adjustment in fuel prices, the utility bills for similar non-solar units, for example, ran about 60 percent more than the Sunscape units.

The first step in energy savings was to minimize the losses through insulation and energy-saving building techniques, Barbash said. While the units were competitively priced with other townhomes in the area, energy-saving features initially added about $1500 to the cost of each unit.

The active and passive solar townhomes took about two years of initial planning with the assistance and cooperation of Brookhaven National Laboratory. The laboratory originally approached local builders to attempt a solar project. Barbash was the only builder interested in the offer. The active solar system and passive features were incorporated into Barbash's existing townhome plans. To record actual energy savings, Brookhaven monitored the project's energy consumption track record.

On the forty-seven-acre site, about twenty-one acres were preserved in their natural state. Units were arranged in a horseshoe pattern around a man-made lake to take advantage of the view and southern exposure.

In 1979, solar water heating was an unpopular option at Hoffman Hills in suburban Chicago. After one year of merchandising, not one solar system was sold.

Solar Sales: Not Always So Hot

The acceptance of active solar systems has faced some cloudy skies in Chicago.

After offering an active solar water-heating option in one of its projects for more than a year, The Hoffman Group Inc. in suburban Chicago was still waiting for its first solar buyer by the fall of 1979. The option was eventually discontinued due to a lack of interest . . . and buyers. "They don't want to pay for it," said Stuart Reich, president of the building firm. "We've had no takers. Zero."

The active solar water-heating system was offered for $4500 at Hoffman Hills, a detached, single-family project in Hoffman Estates, Illinois. Advertising, brochures, displays, and inclusion in a local television station's news special on energy systems failed to produce even one solar buyer.

"We expected solar to be a traffic getter," said vice-president of sales, Don Alexander, "but it didn't do a thing. It's a stiff up-front investment."

Buyers felt that the payback on the active solar investment was too long when the length of homeownership in the area averages only about eight years.

In addition to savings from the federal solar tax credits, the solar system was expected to save the average family about $200 annually, when compared to the cost of operating an electric water-heating system. Estimated savings were calculated by the University of Wisconsin's solar energy laboratory.

Models at Hoffman Hills ranged in price in 1979 from $110,000 to $125,000. The project was designed to include 219 single-family, detached homes on 87 acres.

Solar Hot Water: A Standard Feature with Hot Sales Appeal

Solar energy is one of the best things a builder can do for a home development, according to Jon Hedberg, executive vice president of Hollyfed Inc. in Hollywood, California.

Hollyfed included solar water heating as a standard feature in its Suntree single-family detached homes in Thousand Oaks, California, which opened in June 1979. "We're connecting on a market that other builders haven't taken advantage of," Hedberg said at the time.

The solar offering generated enough buyer excitement to sell 78 units in the first two and a half months of sales. Six models were offered, ranging from $99,950 to $144,000 in price.

Hedberg says that using solar as a marketing tool increased traffic at the project 30 to 40 percent, resulting in the top sales rate in the county at that time. One week they sold seven houses. Hollyfed had already designed their six models for the 183-unit project when they decided to "go solar" and include solar water heating as a standard feature. The addition of solar required no change in roof structure. A solar manufacturer examined the house plans and site plan to approve the project's solar potential.

Solar collectors were placed on the front, back, and garage roofs of the units. The solar system cost, then, about $1750 for equipment and installation. The California 55 percent tax credit was applied to the price tag of the system, bringing the additional cost of the solar system down to about $900. The buyers also qualified for the federal tax credit.

Marketing focused on the solar feature. A billboard reading "Hollyfed presents solar water heating," attracted initially about one hundred and fifty home shoppers. Some publicity resulting from a kick-off visit by Rep. Barry M. Goldwater Jr., R-Calif., resulted in the sale of two houses. Advertisements in local newspapers said, "Solar Power . . . A Ray of Hope for Utility Bills." Most buyers were move-ups, purchasing their second or third homes, Hedberg said.

To avoid future problems, the firm was careful to select a manufacturer with a warranteed system.

Only minor problems occurred during construction, because a local building department did not understand the system. A manufacturer's representative helped explain the system to the department, clearing the way for approval after an eight-week delay.

To avoid delays and installation problems, Hedberg recommended that builders make sure that the manufacturer is reputable and that the installer of the system understands how the collectors integrate with the roof to reduce the chance of leaks.

In the face of local legislation requiring inclusion of solar water heating in homes, Hedberg was glad that his firm was ready. Others, he said, were afraid. The county of San Diego had already passed an ordinance requiring solar water heating in all new construction.

The solar system was estimated to save about 72 percent of the energy needed to heat water. The estimated payback period was about ten years, depending on the lifestyle of the residents. The manufacturer estimated a savings of about $7 per month at that time, when compared to a gas system and $13 per month savings when compared to an electric water-heating system. The manufacturer provided a five-year warranty and annual servicing for the first five years.

Hollyfed planned to build an additional 622-unit, detached development using the same models. With solar? "Definitely," said Hedberg. "We're preparing to make it a part of all of our projects."

Make Savings an Amenity

Most energy-saving features are justified on the basis of direct savings on monthly utility bills. But when such a feature enhances the marketability and livability of the house, the investment indirectly escalates the value of the home as well. It means more than energy savings. It means a nicer home.

In May 1980, builder Bob Schmitt of Strongsville, Ohio, began offering a passive solar amenity in one of his model home plans. The 2236-square-

Hollyfed Inc. offered solar water heating as a standard feature on its single-family detached homes in Thousand Oaks, California. Solar collectors were placed on the front, back, and garage roofs of the units, depending on the house's orientation to the sun. One of the garage-mounted collectors is shown. The project was built in 1979 in response to market demand, without the aid of a grant from HUD.

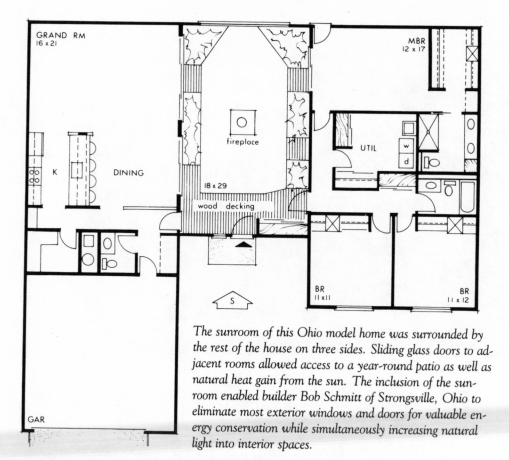

GRAND RM
16 x 21

MBR
12 x 17

fireplace

18 x 29

K

DINING

wood decking

UTIL

w
d

S

BR
11 x 11

BR
11 x 12

GAR

The sunroom of this Ohio model home was surrounded by the rest of the house on three sides. Sliding glass doors to adjacent rooms allowed access to a year-round patio as well as natural heat gain from the sun. The inclusion of the sunroom enabled builder Bob Schmitt of Strongsville, Ohio to eliminate most exterior windows and doors for valuable energy conservation while simultaneously increasing natural light into interior spaces.

foot house was designed around an enclosed garden court. The 600-square-foot sunroom enabled homeowners to cut heating costs by about 50 percent. But it also added valuable living space with a year-round enclosed patio.

The cost of the sunroom amenity in 1980 was $15,500. Schmitt pointed out that the energy savings that result from passive solar heat gain do not justify such an expensive feature. But when combined with increased living space and marketability of a home, the investment takes on another angle. Directly and indirectly, the sunroom saves about 30 percent to 50 percent of the home's heating costs. A typical house with the same square footage would average about $500 per year to heat. The Schmitt model would save about $250 per year, based on 1980 energy prices.

"The investment is only justified by the combination of all of these elements, not just the solar," Schmitt said. "It provides benefits other than heat to make the numbers work." By making the atrium into a year-round patio, the area performed another economical function, he said. The additional space was considered a major amenity.

The sunroom was basically a glass-enclosed garden courtyard with a sun roof and fireplace. The basic advantages of the room were:

- Natural heat gain from the sun;
- Reduced heat loss through windows and doors by orienting them to the atrium rather than exposed to the outside;
- A fireplace which was an amenity as well as an efficient low-cost heat source;
- A year-round patio which was considered a marketing plus in a northern climate.

The atrium served many purposes, both from an economical and visual standpoint. "The essence

Hidden behind the facade of a typical single-family detached house is a twenty-foot by thirty-foot sunroom designed to supply 30 to 50 percent of the heat needed in an Ohio winter.

The sunroom combined energy savings and a year-round patio into a marketable and economical amenity. The fireplace added appeal, while also serving as a supplemental heating source.

of good design is the interrelation of elements," Schmitt said, "not just based on a single facet of the house."

The basic house was priced at $79,973 plus lot in May 1980, including the sunroom. The model was an economized version of a passive plan developed by Schmitt about five years before.

Schmitt said that an active solar system that would heat the house with mechanical equipment would cost at that time about the same for equivalent energy savings. But for the same investment, he thinks that buyers would rather enjoy the amenity too.

In Merchandising Solar, Do Your Homework First

A builder's own homework can be an effective tool in merchandising an energy-efficient house.

At the HeatheRidge development in far-north suburban Chicago, a passive solar townhome model was carefully monitored for three months before the grand opening. The thirty-day monitoring tapes were designed to help the builder determine energy efficiency. But the results were used to show prospective buyers how the house performed under certain test conditions.

Instead of just boasting about energy savings, the builder let the facts speak for themselves. "We don't want to make claims," said Al Bromann, general manager for HeatheRidge Development Co. in Gurnee, Illinois.

The 1300-square-foot, passive solar model was integrated in a four- and eight-plex townhome community at HeatheRidge, ranging in price in early 1981 from $46,000 for an 815-square-foot unit to $83,450 for the two-bedroom, passive solar model.

The footprint for the conventional townhomes and the passive solar townhome was transferable, allowing flexibility to market demand. The firm expected to build four 4-plex passive solar townhome buildings. "Mixing the housing products helps in land planning," Bromann said.

The passive solar unit was priced within $5000 of the price of the other models. Using stan-

dard building materials, the energy-saving features added about $1.50 per square foot in construction costs. Six reservations were made for the passive solar units before the official sales opening in early 1981.

In addition to using the monitoring results as a sales tool in the model, a videotape showed buyers how the house worked. The envelope house was passive solar for heat gain and super-insulated for heat retention. "It takes a long time before the house loses heat," Bromann said.

Inner ceilings were insulated to R19. The outer ceiling was insulated to R30 with a minimum fourteen-inch air space. A greenhouse on the south wall was protected by double-glazed sliding glass doors and R11 wall insulation.

The house included double-wall construction on the northern exposure for maximum protection from cold winter winds. The east, west, and outer north walls were insulated to R26 with 2 inch × 6 inch construction, glass fiber batts and one-inch rigid foam sheathing. A twelve-inch air space was sandwiched between the outer and inner north wall, which was insulated to R11.

But Bromann said that basically the system was not passive solar. "It's geothermal," he said. "We use the earth's natural temperature as a basis for heat." Through use of a crawl space, the system allows the earth's natural 55 degree Fahrenheit temperature to temper the inside air year-round. Natural convection kept the house warm in winter and naturally cooled in summer. In summer, air was cooled by passing through a tube buried seven feet deep in the yard. When the roof of the solarium greenhouse is opened, hot air escapes and cool air is drawn in. Humidity levels in the house ranged between 40 and 60 percent year-round.

The $1500 monitoring system recorded the temperature inside the house, crawl space, greenhouse, and outdoors, through use of remote probes (see photo of recording equipment). Information was recorded on thirty-day sheets. Without use of backup electric baseboard heat, the inside temperature averaged 68 to 72 degrees Fahrenheit during the test period in the winter of 1981, Bromann said. In December 1980, the temperature inside the house never dipped below 58 degrees Fahrenheit. This was true even on days with cloudy

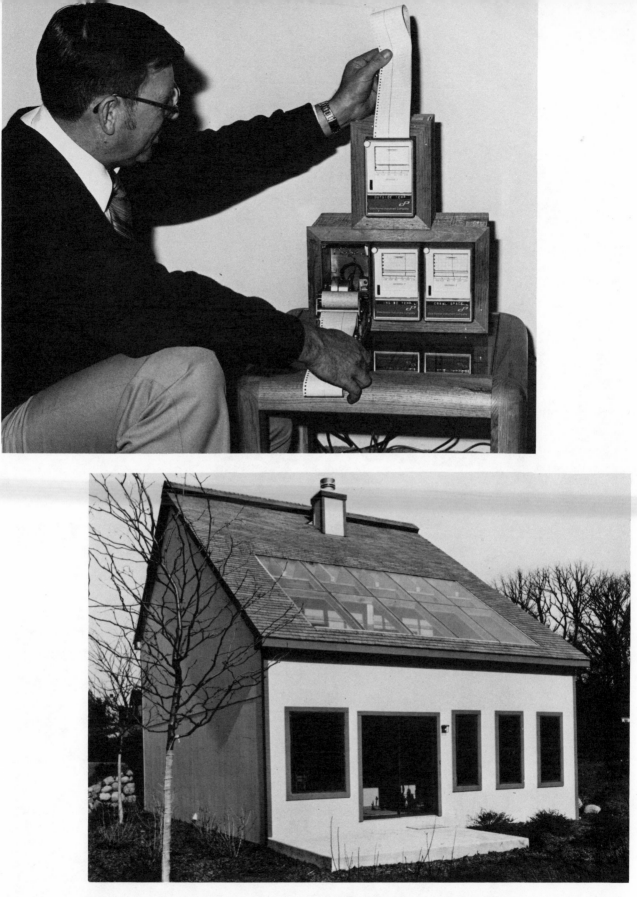

The passive solar townhome model at the HeatheRidge development in Gurnee, Illinois was monitored with temperature probes for three months before the grand opening. The monitoring tapes were used to help show prospective buyers estimated energy savings. The monitoring machine is shown. The exterior photo shows the southern exposure of the monitored unit. The passive solar plan will be incorporated into buildings of four passive solar units attached.

The solarium on the southern exposure of the HeatheRidge townhome was used for aesthetic appeal and for passive solar savings. All rooms in the 1300-square-foot model open onto the solarium.

weather and outside temperatures near zero. Electric baseboard heat was included as a backup heating system. A heat-circulating fireplace was offered as an option.

The firm believes in the savings that can be achieved through passive solar and energy-efficient features. But it remains skeptical about active solar. In 1977, the firm was approached about building a demonstration active solar townhome with a grant. They turned the offer down. "It can't work in Chicago," Bromann said.

But energy efficiency is forefront in the company's plans. "Energy efficiency is very important in merchandising homes," Bromann said. "People are conscious about it. But they are not ready to live in caves."

The passive solar model at HeatheRidge was designed with a greenhouse as part of the passive solar system. All rooms open onto the solarium to take advantage of the benefits of natural heat, light, and cooling. But room orientation to the sunspace also was designed to increase aesthetic appeal. Bromann felt that buyers would be willing to pay extra for the design of the house itself even apart from the energy savings.

In merchandising the model, the builder was careful about what he told buyers about the house's performance. "We realize that the actual energy savings will depend largely on the homeowner," Bromann pointed out.

"We don't want to present it as *the* answer," he said. "But it is a step forward."

Solar technology and passive solar principles work to make solar homes energy-efficient. It was a challenge for builders to make solar cost-efficient too. This passive solar apartment complex in Missouri is one good example.

5

MAKING SOLAR AFFORDABLE

Utility bills have become a significant burden in the homeowner's budget, taking an increasingly big bite out of the family paycheck. Often they rival the cost of the monthly mortgage payment. That has made energy efficiency an important consideration in the home purchase and solar energy a more viable way of keeping down the cost of heating and cooling homes.

Solar systems can make a house more affordable for the homeowner by minimizing monthly utility bills. But affordability encompasses more than monthly savings. The challenge for builders is to make the solar house more affordable for the *buyer* as well.

Construction techniques are one means of developing affordable solar homes. The economics of including an active or passive solar system in a house or development will vary from region to region and will depend largely on the type of the system and its efficiency level. The initial costs will vary as widely as there are different types of equipment and designs. But there are many ways of keeping down these costs. Site-built solar systems, for instance, may cost much less than pre-manufactured ones. Bulk orders from solar manufacturers for an entire solar development can also decrease per-unit costs.

It should be remembered that a solar house does not need to be elaborate or complicated with exotic and expensive equipment in order to be energy efficient. A simple, inexpensive solar system or design can reap big energy savings—whether it is based on active solar equipment, passive solar design, or both.

Active solar water heating is considered one typically easy and cost-effective way to benefit from active solar energy savings. Many builders have included it as a standard or optional feature in their model homes. When priced right, it is an attractive feature for the economy-minded buyer in any market segment from the affordable, attached unit to the custom home.

Reliable solar water-heating systems are considered cost-effective in most areas of the country to supply a portion or all of the home's needs for hot water. Generally, water heating comprises about 15 percent of the homeowner's utility bill. When an active solar water-heating system is combined with water-saving fixtures and well-insulated storage tank and pipes, substantial energy savings can be achieved. An active solar water-heating system can also be combined with either an active solar space-heating system or passive solar design for added energy savings.

The high initial costs of solar equipment are a big challenge. The economics of solar space heating depend on a number of factors including the amount of sunlight in a locality, the expected heating load, the type of equipment, and the size and style of the house.

Although costs and performance levels vary, passive solar heating is usually considered more cost-effective initially than an active solar space-heating system due to the cost of mechanical equipment. But in either type of system, most builders recommend that in order to keep the system cost effective a builder should carefully consider what equipment and components are available locally and what can possibly be fabricated on-site. Careful research into various available systems can lead to the one that is best suited for the particular installation—in cost and performance. As in the automobile industry, solar systems vary from Chevrolet to Mercedes Benz. The system should fit the buyer's needs as well as his pocketbook. An overdesigned system is expensive and unnecessary.

Calculations for long-term payback of the system are generally not considered the best way of determining the affordability of a solar system. Cost considerations should encompass more than initial expenditures and future fuel savings. A good cost analysis should also account for initial construction savings as well, such as the substitution of a south-facing wall with glazing in a passive solar home, or savings in roof covering materials where active solar collectors are placed. Other considerations should also include increased life for conventional HVAC equipment due to decreased heating and cooling loads, and increased resale value of the house in future years. And it is hard to put a price on owner comfort in a solar-heated house.

Experienced builders indicate that most passive solar designs can be implemented with an incremental cost of less than $2000 per home, according to a 1980 market research study conducted by the Drucker Research Co. Inc. of Birmingham, Michigan, and the federally sponsored Solar Energy Research Institute in Golden, Colorado. The study was based on personal interviews with ninety builders, architects, designers, and developers in thirteen major metropolitan areas.

Many builders in the study indicated favorably that passive solar designs are marketable and affordable. They mentioned the following reasons:

- Passive solar concepts appear to be easy to understand.
- Passive solar would require a minimal added cost to constructing a home.
- Homeowners are interested in paying more for energy-efficient homes due to rising utility bills.
- Most passive solar designs use conventional building materials.

- Many designs do not substantially alter the appearance of the building.
- Many passive solar features such as greenhouses can be marketed as amenities.

But even though energy-saving features have become a popular marketing tool, some builders are reluctant to consider passive solar design. Increased levels of insulation and installation of more efficient HVAC equipment are fairly easy to include. But design principles are often overlooked, even though they may be energy efficient and cost effective. Passive solar may mean some changes in the basic house design. But in many cases, the changes are minor and without added cost, such as orienting the house towards a southern exposure and putting most of the windows on that side of the house.

Each experience in solar construction can lead to better and more cost-effective ways of including solar in houses. The first step does not need to be elaborate. It can be as simple and cost effective as re-orienting an energy-efficient house towards the south and increasing glazing on that exposure. The section on solar basics in this book provides many ideas.

Much of successful passive solar construction comes with experience. Builder Chris Delby of Sunstruction Ltd. in the metro-Chicago area told builders who were inexperienced with solar, "Do what I do. Make a mistake and then re-do it." Delby has successfully built at least thirty-five solar houses and retrofitted existing houses to accommodate passive solar design.

Many builders may be reluctant to try solar in their area because they feel that it is really only appropriate in the Southwest. But typical passive solar systems, costing between $2000 and $8000, are economical in most locations, particularly when compared with oil-fired and electric-resistance heating. Solar architect J. Douglas Balcombe and other researchers at Los Alamos Scientific Laboratory collected data on passive solar homes in seven regions in the country and found that annual savings exceeded annual costs in the first year of operation. Simple payback periods averaged eight to twelve years.

The Office of Technology Assessment, which provides Congress with information to evaluate scientific policy, presented studies on several passive solar homes that showed that the measures were economical in areas around the country. Most of the homes surveyed by OTA in the late 1970s were over 50 percent passive solar heated. The OTA report also emphasized marketing factors, stating that a passive solar heating system can increase the value of the home if properly designed, but make the home less desirable if done poorly.

For cost effectiveness, a building or house should be designed climatically for one of the four basic zones: cool, moderate, hot arid, and hot humid. In building a passive solar home, the first thing to ask is, "Can I support this structure naturally?" said solar architect and builder Rodney Wright of the Hawkweed Group in Chicago. That is the most energy and cost-efficient way of building. Between 1973 and 1981, Wright designed and built over one hundred solar buildings and developed an entire solar town in Soldiers Grove, Wisconsin, where every building is dependent on at least half of its heating load provided by the sun.

"Solar is the normal way of building," he said. "That is all it is." He noted that ten out of the fourteen trades needed in building a house are already directly involved in passive solar construction. "No special trades are needed." That means easy adoption of construction techniques by builders and subs—and savings in construction costs.

He admitted that experience is the key to successful solar building. "We've made a lot of mistakes," he said. But through his experience, considering design and building materials, he contends that, "It doesn't cost any more to build passive solar," when compared with conventional construction. A builder, he feels, has an advantage in solar design. "Most systems have been designed by those who didn't know a thing about construction," he said. Cost-efficient solar designs require a working knowledge of construction. Wright suggested that builders consider the entire scope of passive solar systems. "Don't just solve the heating problems," he said. "Work on the others as well, such as cooling, daylighting, and ventilation." All can contribute to the system's cost effectiveness.

Many of the bugs are worked out through hands-on experience. An experienced solar builder remarked to a home builders' association, "It is incredible how much I learned building my first solar house." After his initial experience, he built even more.

But construction experience and the development of cost-efficient building techniques are only one way of making solar an affordable alternative. Most certainly, government-funded demonstrations such as the HUD solar demonstration program helped subsidize solar development and initially make it more affordable for builders to implement and buyers to purchase. But other ways were developed as well. Incentives for builders and buyers of solar homes include grants, low-interest loans, and state and federal tax credits or deductions. Even utility companies have been known to offer cash awards to builders for construction of solar houses. In one program in California, Pacific Gas and Electric Co. provided a $500 award to builder-developers for houses on which reviewers estimated a 50 percent solar contribution, and $1000 if the home design was expected to produce a 75 percent solar contribution.

The tax incentives provide a viable marketing tool for builders. Provided by the state and federal government, they are designed as incentives for buying solar homes by helping reduce the high initial cost of the solar system. The programs were deemed as a good way of stimulating the solar market.

The federal program permits homeowners to deduct from federal taxes 40 percent of the cost of most solar systems to a maximum of $4000. The state government-sponsored credits and deductions are designed for the most part to supplement the federal income tax credit. In most states, the federal tax break can be combined with the state tax incentive for solar homes.

As of mid-1981, forty-five states offered some type of tax break for residential solar systems, in the form of property tax exemption, state income tax credit or deduction, or state sales tax exemption. Some states provide incentives in all three categories. The maximum allowable amounts vary widely from state to state. Some limit the tax break to a dollar amount or a percentage of the cost of the solar system. In some states, exemptions are based on the efficiency or type of the system. Property tax exemptions are sometimes allowable only under a local option. The only states that do not offer any type of tax break are Kentucky, Missouri, Pennsylvania, West Virginia, and Wyoming. The most liberal income tax credits are provided in Arkansas, California, Colorado, Idaho, Indiana, Nebraska, and New Mexico. These states provide up to at least $3000 credit on state income tax or 100 percent deduction of the cost of the system for state income tax purposes. State incentives are designed to make solar systems more attractive by making them more affordable.

But unfortunately, although these tax breaks can make a big difference in the real cost of a solar system, many of these incentives have been ignored by builders and have gone largely unnoticed by home buyers. In 1980, about 52 percent of consumers indicated that they were unaware of federal and state solar energy tax credits, according to a survey conducted by the Opinion Research Corporation. The survey also revealed that 60 percent of consumer/homeowners said that they would be more likely to consider buying a solar energy system if a significant tax credit was available. Survey results were derived from over 2000 personal interviews and 1680 telephone interviews among consumers.

These results were echoed in a 1981 survey of over 2000 homeowners and 4000 solar homeowners by the Solar Energy Research Institute. The report noted that while the tax credits were designed to promote solar use, 54 percent of the respondents were unaware that the federal government provided a solar tax credit and 56 percent did not know whether or not their states provided solar tax credits.

Tax incentives can greatly reduce the initial cost of solar for buyers. That is a marketing opportunity largely missed by builders. It is a way of making solar even more affordable for the home buyer.

In addition to the tax credit programs, another means of making solar housing more affordable was developed by the Department of Housing and Urban Development. Recognizing the impact of energy savings in solar homes, mortgages insured by the Federal Housing Authority were allowed to exceed the maximum allowable amounts up to 20 percent if the housing unit includes a solar energy system, according to HUD. The regulation allows an increase up to 20 percent more than currently authorized mortgages for residences which include energy-saving solar systems. The increase in allowable mortgage amounts was expected to help cover the added cost of the solar system and encourage the use of solar energy in housing units.

FHA-insured mortgages for both existing structures and new construction were eligible for the increase if they incorporate wind or solar energy systems to reduce dependence on other energy sources.

The ability of homeowners to meet their monthly payments is a big concern among lenders. As the cost of utilities continues to rise, the monthly costs of heating a home have become an increasingly important factor in determining the affordability of a home. As a result, energy efficiency has become a consideration in qualifying buyers for a mortgage.

A solar home may make the home not only more affordable to own, but more affordable to buy.

Almost 60 percent of lenders take energy efficiency into consideration on mortgage loan applications, according to a 1981 survey conducted by The Mortgage Corporation on the impact of energy efficiency in lending. But at the same time, about 90 percent of the lenders said that consideration did not necessarily imply that energy-efficient or solar homes were given preferential treatment. Energy efficiency is a consideration, not a free ticket.

In the appraisal process, 68 percent of the lenders in the survey said that their staff and fee appraisers have been instructed to consider energy costs and efficiency. Solar systems are recognized for increasing the energy efficiency of the home. About 84 percent of the lenders will grant loans for active solar energy systems and 81 percent will grant loans for passive solar energy systems. But borrowers are informed about energy lending programs by only about 29 percent of the lender/respondents.

"Many lenders indicated their concern about the effect that energy costs will have upon the ability of borrowers to meet their monthly mortgage obligations," The Mortgage Corporation report concluded. High energy costs have been identified by about 12 percent of the lenders as the cause for delinquencies and foreclosures.

For the most part, lenders and The Mortgage Corporation look quite favorably on houses that require less energy to operate. In its underwriting guidelines, The Mortgage Corporation defines what constitutes an energy-efficient property in an appraisal report. These factors are taken into consideration in the mortgage application. An energy-efficient home, in its estimation, includes "cost-efficient design, materials, equipment, and site orientation in providing conservation of non-renewable fuels." These items include: insulation; caulking and weatherstripping; double and triple glazed windows; window shading or landscaping for solar control; automatic setback thermostats; HVAC equipment and home appliances designed for energy efficiency; solar systems for water heating, space heating and cooling; wood-fired heating systems; and building designs which minimize energy use, such as those using smaller window areas and earth sheltering.

"Increasing energy costs should be of concern to borrowers and lenders alike," The Mortgage Corp. states. It notes that special energy-efficient items should be recognized in the appraisal process. Their importance is recognized since, "any increase in principal and interest payments resulting from these items being included in the financing may be offset or exceeded by the savings in energy costs."

The affordability of a solar home is based on construction and marketing principles. Initial costs, energy savings, tax credits, and buyer qualification must all be balanced. Affordability means a combination of cost-efficient construction practices as well as the ability of a builder to use tax credits and favorable lender attitudes to market the home to prospective buyers.

On the following pages, builders across the country show how, in their own ways, they have made solar an affordable alternative.

The Challenge: Make It Passive Solar and Keep It Affordable

Building an affordable passive solar house presented Hess Home Builders Inc. of Lancaster, Pennsylva-

nia, with more than a challenge. It provided the firm with a marketing edge.

In the past, Hess's models drew about six couples out on a typical Sunday afternoon. But its 1546-square-foot, passive solar model, which sold for $52,500 without land, drew a crowd of 3,500 in the first three weeks of an open house in late November 1980. By February 1981, the house still attracted about 300 people per weekend.

Most passive solar houses that I saw tended to be over $100,000, said designer Donald White of Hess Home Builders Inc. The public's reaction was that "solar is just too expensive." Using his experience in designing and building two previous large, passive solar houses, White designed a more affordable model. Many of the same keys in keeping a conventional house affordable must be used in keeping down the cost of a passive solar house.

First, White said, the size of the house must be kept small. Hallways should be eliminated wherever possible and living areas grouped together to maximize use of space and make the house look larger.

The size and layout of the house also help keep the house more energy efficient. The one-and-a-half to two-story, open design with cathedral ceiling and loft also maximizes the circulation of heat and natural cooling. The model was built on concrete slab, eliminating the cost of constructing a basement. In 1980, construction costs for the model were about $35 per square foot, excluding land.

White was surprised, and pleased, with the buyer response. In the first two months, two houses were sold and twenty-three more were in the design stage. The model only served as a base for other designs. Some buyers made modifications, such as adding a garage or changing the floor plan. The houses ranged from $46,000 to $95,000 (without land) in 1980. Most averaged about $60,000, depending on the plan and options.

The passive solar model affected the firm's business. Out of the twenty-six houses White was designing in early 1981 for customers, only two were not solar.

As a result of the passive solar model, White felt that the firm has a leg up on the competition. Out of the 130 registered home builders in the

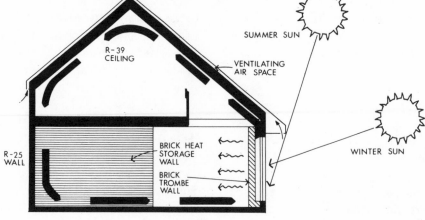

SUMMER SUN

VENTILATING
AIR SPACE

R-39
CEILING

WINTER SUN

R-25
WALL

BRICK HEAT
STORAGE
WALL

BRICK
TROMBE
WALL

142

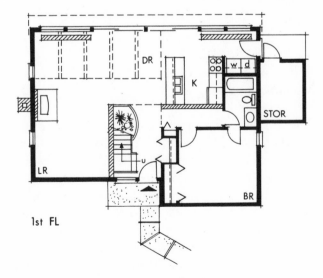

1st FL

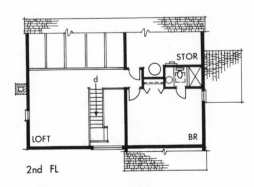

2nd FL

In the passive solar model house built by Hess Home Builders Inc. of Lancaster, Pennsylvania, windows on the north, east, and west exposures were kept to a minimum and glazed areas maximized on the southern exposure, as shown in the exterior photos.

The interior featured a cathedral ceiling and loft for natural convection of heating and cooling. The schematic shows how the convection loop was designed to operate in the house. In late 1980, the 1546-square-foot model sold for $52,500 excluding land.

143

county, only three or four even expressed an interest in solar. Hess was the first to go out and actually build one, White said.

"And that provided us with a marketing edge," he added. "We were the first to build solar in that price range. And our model was the first that the people in the community saw." Many of the sales, he noted, have resulted from referrals— good old word-of-mouth advertising. "Energy is really on people's minds," he said.

White said that passive solar design really involves only two simple steps: proper orientation of the house and extra glazing on the southern exposure to take advantage of solar heat gain.

When compared to a similar conventional house, the passive solar model cost about an extra $900 for additional glazing and $2500 for the construction of a trombe wall directly inside the glazing on the southern exposure. An interior brick wall also was included to absorb excess heat.

To help keep down the extra costs, White investigated the most inexpensive way to glaze the southern elevation. He used two 8-foot patio doors and additional pieces of fixed glass on that exposure. By using standard building materials, his method cost only about one-third of the cost of additional glazing, he said. He considered installing quarry tile on the floor to help absorb direct heat gain, but he could not justify the extra $3500 cost.

But as the house was designed, sun power alone provided about 40 percent of the needed heat. A wood stove was able to heat the entire house. "The house can operate without using electricity for heat at all," White said.

But although the house could be self-sufficient, mortgage companies required that White include an electric baseboard heating system as a backup source. Due to the reduced heating load, however, a conventional heating system was installed 30 percent smaller than typically needed in a house of that size.

Estimated savings for the model were calculated by the local utility. At 1980 utility costs, the annual heating bill was estimated to be $257 for the 1546-square-foot house, *without* consideration of solar heat gain or the wood stove. A conventional house with the same square footage was estimated to cost about $450 per year to heat.

To measure actual performance, temperature readings were taken. The second floor of the house ranged within a couple of degrees of the temperature on the first floor. White said that indicates there is no heat stratification and that the convection loop operates properly, naturally circulating the heat throughout the house.

Insulation was a big factor in the house's heating efficiency. "Insulation keeps the heat from the sun *inside* the house," White said. Ceilings were insulated to R39. Walls were insulated to R25 with 2 × 6 construction. Insulated exterior doors with a magnetic weather seal provided R15.5. Double-insulated glass was used on the southern exposure for maximum heat gain. Overhangs were designed to keep the glazed areas shaded in summer. Triple-glazed windows were used on the other three exposures. Windows on those exposures were kept to a minimum to reduce heat loss. Wall projections were designed to help shield the entry and minimize air infiltration.

The $52,500 price tag for the model also included a $2,600 active solar water-heating system.

To heat the entire house with an active solar system, White pointed out, would cost in excess of $15,000. "Without a doubt, passive solar is the most cost-effective way to energy efficiency," he said.

A Passive Solar Sunspace in a Manufactured House

Passive solar was long recognized as a design alternative that could help reduce the high cost of heating a home. But passive solar relies on design rather than mechanical equipment to absorb the sun's natural heat. That often means building a custom home in order to include passive solar techniques or conducting expensive design alterations to an existing plan. But in 1980, Mayhill Homes Corp. of Gainesville, Georgia, incorporated these design concepts into a manufactured house.

About 20 percent of Mayhill's housing stock will be passive solar by 1990, predicted John Odegaard, vice-president of Mayhill product development. In 1980, Mayhill produced about 1200 manufactured homes.

ESTIMATED HEATING CONTRIBUTION FOR VARIOUS CITIES

The following percentages of the home's heating needs were calculated by the Southern Solar Energy Center in Atlanta, Georgia. The center warns that in the starred locations, extra care must be taken to prevent overheating in summer.

City	% Solar
Akron	22
Asheville	46
Atlanta	53
Birmingham	54
Cape Hatteras	59
Charleston*	70
Charlotte	57
Chicago	27
Cleveland	21
Columbia	61
Columbus	25
Covington	22
Fort Wayne	23
Gainesville, FL*	90
Greenville/ Spartanburg	59
Indianapolis	27
Jacksonville*	85
Louisville	31
Macon	68
Memphis	49
Mobile*	79
Montgomery	66
Norfolk	47
Orlando*	90
Raleigh/ Durham	55
Richmond	42
Roanoke	40
St. Louis	36
Savannah*	78
South Bend	22
Tallahassee*	82
Tampa*	90

The passive solar plan was designed to provide from 21 percent to 90 percent of the home's winter heating needs, depending on location (see chart). These estimates were based on calculations made by the Southern Solar Energy Center in Atlanta, Georgia. The first model was a 1788-square-foot, single-family, detached plan including a 250-square-foot solarium. It was available with or without the $2024 solar design option. The total package price for the home, including the solar option, was $18,924 in 1980, excluding land, freight, taxes, and interior and exterior finish. The builder was also responsible for providing 55-gallon drums for use as a storage medium, grills for return air ducts, and a masonry foundation.

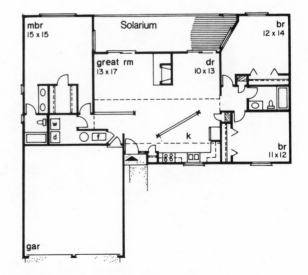

Mayhill's floor plan for it's single-family passive solar model. Copyrighted by Mayhill Homes Corporation.

Mayhill's first passive solar model was constructed and tested for performance in Asheville, North Carolina. The 1788-square-foot, copyrighted plan was designed to provide from 21 percent to 90 percent of the home's winter heating needs. The front and back elevations are shown, as well as the interior of the sunspace on the rear elevation (right).

Mayhill's passive solar system used a glass exterior wall to form a solarium on the rear elevation of the unit. Facing a southern exposure, this enclosure was designed to trap natural heat gain. According to Odegaard, the advantages of the solarium as a passive solar design technique are:

- making it look like part of the house by recessing it;
- reducing heat loss by exposing fewer exterior walls to the weather;
- providing more rooms with direct access to a greenhouse space;
- making it easier to build by only having to erect one glass wall;
- shielding the living room carpet and furniture from damaging sunlight;
- allowing the house itself to provide the structural elements for the greenhouse.

The solarium design option ranged from $1800 to $3400 depending on the size of the house. The package included: single-glazed panels (glass with a wood frame), an operating window sash with sunscreen shades, all fasteners, foundation vents, the drum room enclosure, and a rust inhibitor for the drums. Water was used as a storage medium in 55-gallon drums, obtained by the builder locally for about $4 to $8 per drum. It is a virtually costless storage system, said Odegaard.

Excess heat is absorbed by about fifteen drums of water located in a storage area behind a glazed

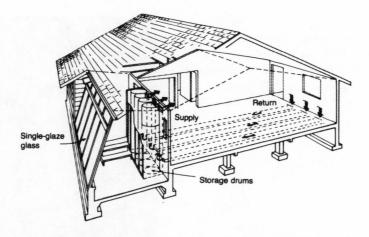

The house is heated in winter through use of natural convection, or a thermosyphon loop. Heated air in the sunspace and drum storage area is circulated throughout the house. Copyrighted by Mayhill Homes Corporation.

plastic wall. In the winter, the house is heated by a thermosyphon loop. Heated air is circulated through ducts and sliding glass doors into the home (see schematic drawing). In summer, moveable shades, windows, and vents help keep the solarium from becoming overheated. An aluminum awning window provides shade also to help reduce any overheating problems in summer.

As a design amenity, access to the solarium was provided through sliding glass doors from the master bedroom, a secondary bedroom, the great room, and the dining room.

In November 1980, Mayhill began marketing three additional copyrighted single-family detached plans with the solar design option. These homes ranged in size from 1216 square feet to 2030 square feet. The solarium location on the four models varied from the rear or side elevation for design flexibility on the home site.

Expandable Plan Offers Low-Priced Solar Heating

An affordable solar house *can* be a simple task. And that is the key: keep it simple. But an affordable house also needs to be marketable with features that consumers want, said builder R. B. Fitch of Carrboro, North Carolina.

The result was a 1690-square-foot, contemporary house, including an expandable, unfinished second level and a simple solar system that stores heat in water-filled, plastic milk containers.

Built for about $31 per square foot, the house sold for $77,500 in early 1979, including the finished second level and land. Without land, the same house would have cost about $63,000 at that

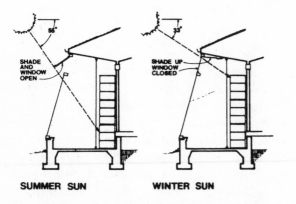

An awning window was designed to help reduce overheating in the summer. The window in the open position in summer provides shade and ventilation. Copyrighted by Mayhill Homes Corporation.

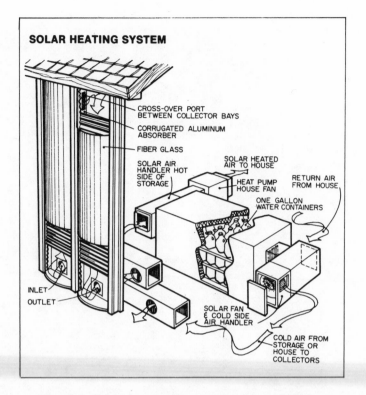

SOLAR HEATING SYSTEM

CROSS-OVER PORT
BETWEEN COLLECTOR BAYS

CORRUGATED ALUMINUM
ABSORBER

FIBER GLASS

SOLAR AIR
HANDLER HOT
SIDE OF
STORAGE

SOLAR HEATED
AIR TO HOUSE

HEAT PUMP
HOUSE FAN

RETURN AIR
FROM HOUSE

ONE GALLON
WATER CONTAINERS

INLET

OUTLET

SOLAR FAN
& COLD SIDE
AIR HANDLER

COLD AIR FROM
STORAGE OR
HOUSE TO
COLLECTORS

*The schematic of the solar heating system shows how the
sun-warmed air travels from the collector through the storage box containing gallon plastic containers filled with
water.*

time, including a finished third bedroom and bath which cost about $5000, a two-car garage for about $5760, and materials and installation of the solar heating system for about $5000. The house plans were designed in conjunction with the American Plywood Association and *Family Circle* magazine.

The house features a simple and inexpensive solar heating system designed to provide about 50 percent of the space heating for the home. "The basic idea was to present solar heating in an economical fashion," said architect Jon Condoret.

Materials for the system were available locally, costing about $2000 to $2500. The system was designed for builders to construct on-site themselves. Collectors were fabricated from corrugated aluminum sheets painted black, covered with a fiberglass glazing (see schematic). The collectors were located on the wall facing south.

The only moving part was a fan that circulated the air through the collectors and an in-

sulated storage box in the crawl space containing 550 gallon plastic containers filled with water and stacked three high. The sun-warmed air moves through the storage box where the water absorbs excess heat, storing enough heat for one to two sunless days. Backup heat is supplied by a heat pump.

The plastic containers, used typically as milk bottles, were purchased from local suppliers for about 15 cents a piece. Glass bottles would work as well, but the plastic was found to be far more economical, said solar designer Craig Fitzpatrick. The whole idea behind the simple solar system was to make solar heating more affordable for the average home buyer, the architect added.

Two years after the house was sold, no complaints or problems had been reported by the owners. Actual savings were not monitored.

According to architect Condoret, the house design could also work without the collectors. In-

North Carolina builder R. B. Fitch built a contemporary house with affordability and solar in mind. The 1690-square-foot, expandable plan included an unfinished second level for a future third bedroom and bath. Solar collectors were located on the rear elevation, oriented to the south. PHOTOS: American Plywood Association.

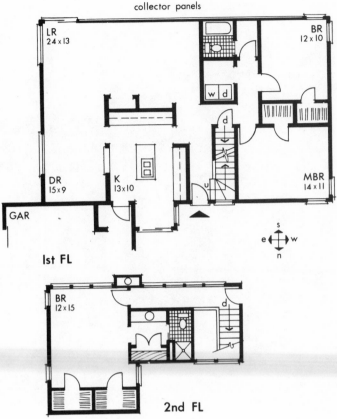

stead, glazed window areas could be added to the south-facing wall for passive solar heat gain.

Builder Fitch also included energy savers such as R17-insulated walls and R19 to R30 ceiling insulation, double-glazed windows, double-domed skylights, an open plenum wood foundation, a ceiling fan, caulking and weatherstripping, and steel-insulated entry doors.

The basic plan included 1256 square feet of living space on the first level with two bedrooms and one bath. An unfinished bedroom and bath on the second level added 440 square feet to accommodate a growing family, and a two-car garage measured 480 square feet. Not including the garage or a seven-foot by four-foot breakfast nook, the house only measured 28 feet by 44 feet. "A contemporary home is inherently expandable," Fitch said.

Affordability required keeping construction costs as low as possible, but it also called for careful consideration of the floor plan. "We tried to make the house functional, designing the most living space possible within the small area," said architect Condoret. Important features in the floor plan included a good traffic pattern and the elimination of corridor space as much as possible.

Passive Solar Modular Designs Combine Cost Effectiveness and Energy Efficiency

Passive solar designs can help make a house more affordable after the sale by maximizing the home's potential for energy savings. For the low end of the housing market, reduced heating bills can make all the difference in helping homeowners meet monthly housing payments.

In an effort to encourage low-cost passive solar designs, the Tennessee Valley Authority supplied technical and financial assistance in 1980 to

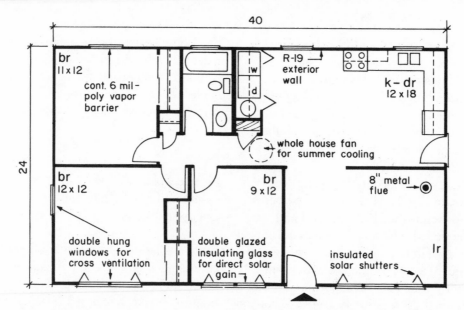

The 960-square-foot Sunburst model was designed by Dixie Royal Homes of Cooke-ville, Tennessee, under a passive solar, modular homes program sponsored by the Tennessee Valley Authority. Note on the floor plan that the living area and bedrooms were arranged along the southern exposure of the house to take advantage of natural heat gain.

five home manufacturers to produce modular, passive solar designs. The program was authorized in 1979. Designs were completed and produced by mid-1981.

The five manufacturers were: Dixie Royal Homes Inc. of Cookeville, Tennessee, Guerdon Industries of Louisville, Kentucky, Monroe Modular Homes of Madisonville, Tennessee, Panel-Fab of Miami, Florida, and the Eastern Kentucky Housing Development Corp. of Neon, Kentucky.

In focusing on low-cost housing, "our aim was to keep the cost as low as possible while increasing energy efficiency," said Kris Ballal, a solar consultant who worked with Dixie Royal Homes, one of the recipients of the TVA awards. The firm was the first to produce a passive solar model under the program.

The result was the modular Sunburst model which retailed for less than $20,000 in late 1980, excluding freight, set-up, land, and landscaping. The model was only one of the passive solar designs that Dixie Royal Homes produced under the program.

Passive solar features in the model included south-facing windows, natural ventilation, and extra insulation. The extra passive solar and energy-conserving features added an estimated $1500 to the cost of the home. But the investment shows in the savings. An independent firm estimated that the unit would save about 76 percent on heating costs and 25 percent on cooling the unit, when compared with TVA's Super Saver design standards.

Under the passive solar program, the manufacturers were required to produce designs that would save at least 50 percent of the energy needed to heat a house built under TVA Super Saver standards. The Super Saver houses were used as the base for comparing the savings achieved under the passive solar program. Specifications for the Super Saver homes included: R19 wall and floor insulation, R30 ceiling insulation, a vapor barrier, double-glazed windows, and no more than 10 percent of the house's square footage in glazed areas.

The 960-square-foot, Sunburst model included three bedrooms, one bath, living room, and kitchen. To make the most of natural solar heat gain, living areas and bedrooms were located on the southern exposure (see plan). To reduce heat loss through glazed areas at night, thermal shutters were also included. In summer months, a whole-house attic fan was designed to aid in natural ventilation.

Conventional energy-saving features in the Sunburst design included: R19 wall insulation, R38 ceiling insulation, a continuous vapor barrier, caulking, weatherstripping, and thermal-pane storm windows. Passive solar heat gain was supplemented by electric baseboard heating units. The model was equipped also with flues for wood-burning stove installations.

The TVA passive solar modular homes program funded 130 prototype passive solar homes throughout its seven-state service area. Twenty designs were electronically monitored twenty-four hours a day by TVA to determine actual energy savings. The other 110 prototype houses, built from the twenty basic designs, were metered for energy savings. TVA provided the buyers of the prototype homes with $1000 in exchange for monitoring privileges for one year.

The 130 completed houses each were held open to the public for two consecutive weekends for use as an educational tool. "Education is just part of the development of a passive solar market," said Rolland Holt, project manager of the TVA solar program. "The goal of the program is to prove whether or not there is a market for passive solar," Holt said. "These are not experimental homes. They provide livable floor plans for a price-conscious market. . . . If there is to be a meaningful impact with solar, it has to be cost-effective."

According to Holt, the major objective of the program was for TVA to work with profit-oriented producers of housing to combine TVA technical support with the manufacturers' production expertise. The goal was to develop cost-effective, energy-efficient homes.

The TVA program was designed to provide some of the capital needed to experiment with passive solar construction methods and to help speed up the learning process. Each manufacturer received an award averaging about $225,000 to hire solar consultants and to cover the cost of the house design, open houses, incentives, and the cost of building the prototypes. Funding for the $2.9 million TVA program was distributed among the home manufacturers, TVA administrators, and to cover the cost of the monitoring equipment.

Including panelized and sectional housing, the passive solar designs were expected to be priced between the low $20,000s and upper $30,000s, so that home buyers could qualify for existing governmental programs, such as the Federal Housing Administration, Veterans Administration, and Farmers Home Administration mortgage financing programs.

"We are not subsidizing exotic designs," Holt emphasized. "The house designs must be cost effective to meet this market's demand."

Each of the twenty designs, Holt said, approached passive solar in a slightly different way, ranging from direct gain to sunspaces to storage mass. "The program focuses on what is *really* cost effective in practice, not just in theory," Holt said. "Many techniques work out from a thermal performance standpoint, but do not pencil out in cost effectiveness."

The manufacturers found that it was comparatively simple to meld passive solar into production designs, Holt said. "Passive solar is just one technique to reduce energy consumption. We can't ignore energy conservation methods in light of new technology."

"We need to couple-up energy-saving features and passive solar to reduce the heating and cooling load to a reasonable level and then utilize passive solar to carry part of the balance," Holt said. Over and above the cost of tightening up the house, the passive solar features were estimated to add about $1000 to $5000 to the cost of construction, depending on the house size and design. Surprisingly, it was not necessary to get too exotic in order to cut energy costs, Holt said.

After producing the 130 prototype houses from the 20 basic designs, the manufacturers were expected to incorporate the passive solar houses within their standard housing lines. Once in regular production, manufacturers will determine which designs are the most marketable and acceptable. Buyer response determines how many more of the homes will be built, Holt said.

"The program will be a success," Holt said, "*if* the buyers want the passive solar designs . . . and will buy them."

In addition to working with the manufacturers, TVA conducted educational programs for realtors, home builders' associations, financing agencies, and appraisers.

"The program was not just designed to speed up the construction of the passive solar homes," Holt said. "We're dealing with a real world and all facets are needed in order to open up the market."

Active Solar Heat Can Make Housing Even More Affordable

Reduced energy costs and affordable housing go hand-in-hand, according to developer Harry Watson of Projects Unlimited Inc. in Irvine, California. With a single newspaper advertisement in June 1980, he sold out the first phase of forty-eight active solar condominiums in the first three weeks of sales without models. The two- and three-bedroom units were priced from $62,000 to $67,000. The units included solar water heating and space heat as standard features. "There is an incredible demand for affordable housing," Watson said.

But affordability affects energy costs as well. Utility costs for the units were included in the monthly maintenance fee, adding only about $10 per month for hot water and space heat on an annual basis.

The 240-unit Autumn Heights condominium project in San Marcos, California, was Watson's first solar venture. It resulted largely from a San Diego County ordinance that required solar water heating to be included in new developments, effective on new construction as of October 1980.

Watson was skeptical at first about the high costs of developing a solar project. He admits that the solar construction requirement almost convinced him to not build, but to sell the land.

Then, in searching for solutions, he investigated low-cost solar systems. The active solar system he selected to use in the project was developed

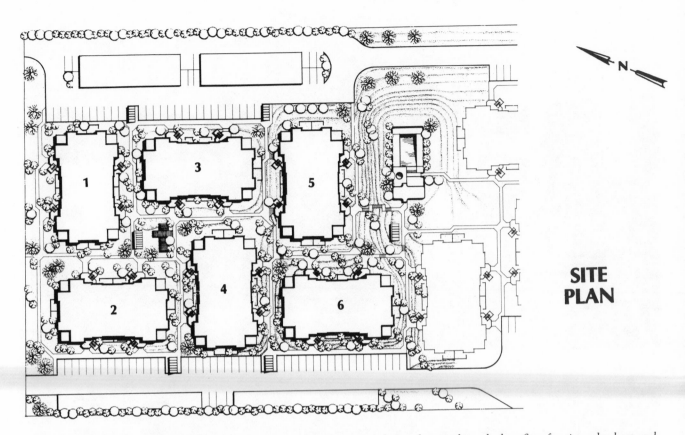

SITE PLAN

Harry Watson's solar condominium development near San Diego was designed to combine the benefits of active solar heat and hot water with affordable housing. The two- and three-bedroom stacked units were priced from $62,000 to $67,000 in June 1980. (See photos on next page.)

by Piper Hydro Inc. of Anaheim, California. The system only added about $3 per square foot in hard construction costs. It was estimated to reduce energy costs by about 82 percent, Watson said.

One advantage of a multifamily solar project was that the mechanical solar equipment and collectors could be centralized, supplying heat and hot water for many units, rather than just an individual unit or house. The solar collectors were located in remote arrays throughout the development in energy centers adjacent to the parking sheds (see photo on next page).

The collectors operate without the high temperatures and pressure typically related to breakdowns in solar equipment. The solar heat was transferred hydronically between the energy centers and the 16-unit buildings through a continuous

loop of insulated copper tubing buried underground. A gas-fired boiler in each of the energy centers was included to supply backup heating, if needed.

Because of the continuous hydronic loop system, if any section of the solar or backup heating equipment was not functioning, heat was still transferred to all of the units without interruption.

Another benefit of the energy centers was that no square footage was required to enclose water heaters or furnaces in each of the units, providing more living space in the 1100-square-foot and 1190-square-foot stacked condominium units. Also, the architecture and siting of the buildings was unaffected by the inclusion of solar collectors.

As a result of the project, Watson became sold on solar. He committed his future develop-

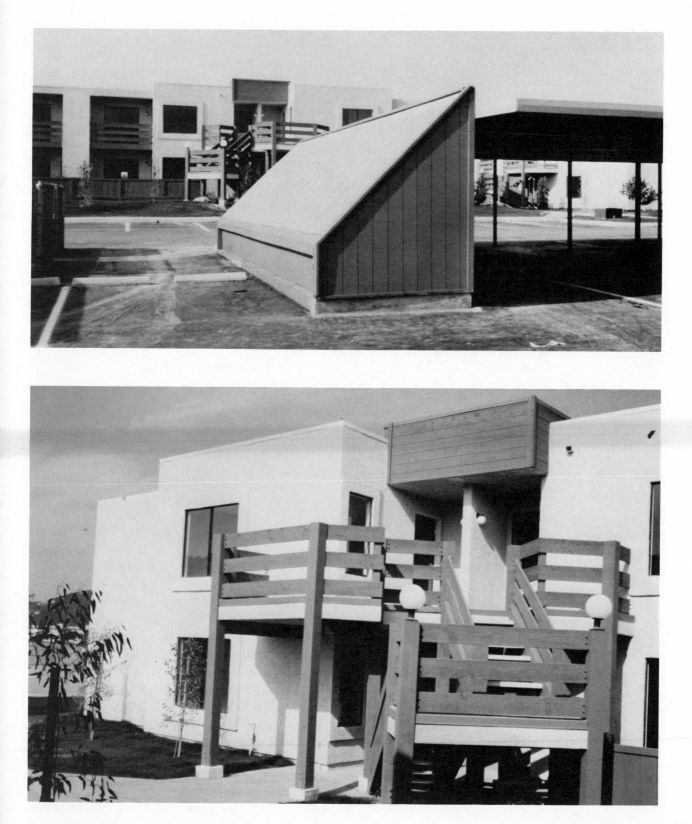

Solar collectors and backup heating equipment were located in energy centers scattered throughout the development. Solar heat was transferred hydronically through a buried, insulated copper tubing loop. PHOTOS: Jeff Bates.

ments to include similar solar systems. Autumn Heights was only the first, he said. Others include a 192-unit solar condominium project in Colorado Springs, Colorado, which sold 19 units without models. An additional 300 solar condominium units in California began construction in February 1981.

Passive Solar Apartments: High Occupancies for the Builder, Low Utility Bills for the Tenant

Energy savings increased rental income for builder Gary Lambeth of Lambeth Properties Inc. in Springfield, Missouri.

By building passive solar features into 109 apartments at Strawberry Fields West in early 1980, Lambeth was able to reduce his tenants' monthly utility costs. But at the same time, the features enabled him to command higher rents.

Economically, the cost to the tenant worked out to remain about the same. But instead of the money going to the utility company, it was directed to the apartment owner—Lambeth. It was a simple balance between higher rents and cheaper utilities. The tenant obtained a nicer apartment for about the same basic monthly cost. "I can charge higher rents because the tenants are paying less on utilities," Lambeth said.

In 1980, the passive solar units saved about $10 to $15 per month on utility costs when compared to other apartments in the area. Lambeth increased his rents to make up the difference in the tenants' monthly costs. Utilities for the passive solar apartments were estimated at about $26 per month in early 1980. Rents for the one and two bedroom units ranged, then, from $200 to $230 per month.

The passive solar features were designed to save about 30 percent on utility bills in the winter and 10 to 15 percent in the summer, Lambeth said.

For proper passive solar siting, the buildings were constructed on a ridge running east and west. Passive solar features included: orientation of window areas to the southern exposure, minimal window area on the northern exposure, vertical vanes

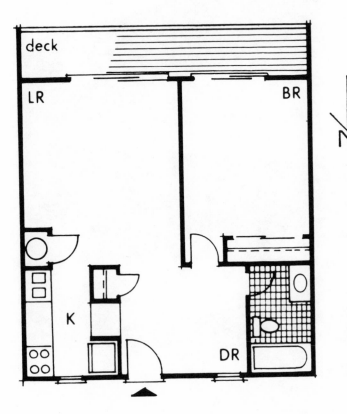

Strawberry Fields West, a passive solar apartment project in Springfield, Missouri, commanded higher rents due to a reduction in the tenants' monthly utility bills. The project included one-bedroom (shown here) and two-bedroom models.

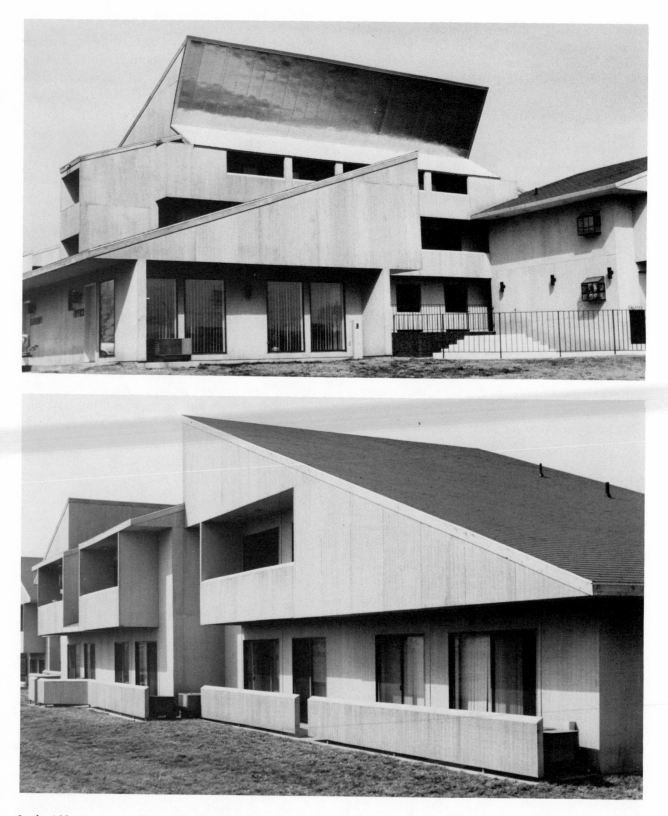

In the 109 apartments of Strawberry Fields West, large window areas were oriented to the south for natural heat gain.
PHOTOS: Jim Mayfield and James Lambeth.

on south-facing sliding glass doors to reduce heat loss at night, R26 wall insulation, R40 ceiling insulation, electric heat pumps, and double-glazed windows and sliding glass doors.

Lambeth admitted that it cost about 7 to 8 percent more to build passive solar into the apartments. But he also felt that he obtained a better return on his investment as a result. "There was an increase in costs," he noted, "but also an increase in value."

The passive solar design and features save energy. But it also appealed to his young professional market. As a result, he boasted the highest occupancies in the area. Lambeth considered the bold design and energy savings as the project's strongest calling cards. "The cleanliness of the design," he felt, "adds to the overall appearance of the project."

Although it looks like an active solar collector, the highly angled roof design on the clubhouse was included only for aesthetic purposes. Lambeth did not feel that active solar collectors were economical to include at the time of construction. But the design is adaptable for inclusion of solar collectors when it is deemed feasible in the future (see photo on page 135).

The entire project includes about 300 apartments on 30 acres. All apartments that Lambeth's firm builds are retained for his own investment.

By using in-house construction, design, and development services, Lambeth was also able to save about 20 to 25 percent in construction costs. "It provides the edge over other developers in the area," Lambeth said.

Lambeth's firm also manages the apartments. And Lambeth pointed out that cost efficiencies are what make an apartment project profitable. "Profitability comes from the gross savings of handling everything ourselves," he said. And a fully occupied project doesn't hurt.

Solar has progressed from strictly custom, one-of-a-kind homes to encompass production housing from standard plans such as this model home located in suburban Sacramento, California.

6

SOLAR AS A
STANDARD MODEL

Many builders question whether they can afford to include solar features or equipment in their standard tract homes. But many are beginning to question whether they can afford not to. Buyers demand energy efficiency in homes, and solar is one viable means of fulfilling that need.

The economics of solar investments are becoming more attractive as the cost of conventional utilities increases. Cost-effective solar energy is emerging from the realm of science fiction and becoming a reality in production housing, according to one industry source.

The image of solar is changing in the minds of builders. Just as solar systems and designs have evolved, builders' attitudes towards the inclusion of solar in model homes are changing. As consumers become more aware of their benefits, solar energy systems are becoming a serious consideration among builders as standard or optional features in their model homes.

Energy efficiency is a big concern in the eyes of builders. In a 1980 study by *Professional Builder* magazine, 76.4 percent of builders surveyed said that they believe that the energy crisis is real. Builders do not expect energy problems to vanish. About 87 percent perceived that the crisis is serious and will have long-term consequences.

Energy shortages and high utility bills have caused builders to examine the options. As a result, many builders are gaining in solar experience. Of the builders surveyed by *Professional Builder*, 12 per-

cent reported that in 1980 they were currently building or built at least one active solar home in the previous twelve months. Only 9.2 percent of builders surveyed had solar experience in mid-1978 and only 8.2 percent of those polled in mid-1977. Builders were not questioned in regards to their experience in passive solar construction in those particular surveys.

Overall, builders are becoming less skeptical about the potential of solar as a viable source of heat for homes. Their reservations about solar systems have decreased dramatically since mid-1978. Only about half of builders had reservations about solar systems in the 1980 report, compared with 82.7 percent in the mid-1978 study. The difference in builder attitudes was quite pronounced, as noted in this comparative chart.

Builder Reservations	1980	Mid-1978
High initial cost	42.1%	80.0%
Savings not documented	0	45.9
Unavailable equipment	7.9	35.6
Subcontractors can't handle	2.6	35.1
Inappropriate climate	18.4	33.2
Appearance	0	19.9
Other	29.0	12.5

SOURCE: *Professional Builder*

Solar has definitely gained a more positive image over the years. And builders have become much more sensitive to the potential of solar systems as a part of increasing energy efficiency in the homes they build.

In a 1981 *Professional Builder* study, builders were questioned about how they had increased the energy efficiency of home mechanical HVAC equipment in the previous two years. Of those polled, 22.5 percent said that they had designed in more passive solar features and 6.7 percent had included active solar systems. Those results were even more pronounced in the north central region of the United States where 42.1 percent said they included more passive solar features and 15.8 percent had incorporated active solar systems.

In the *Professional Builder* study, most builders indicated that they consider active solar energy systems a viable alternative source of energy in their regions. Survey results indicated that 9 percent definitely believed in solar and had actually built a solar home, 19.1 percent said that they plan to build solar in the near future, and 55.1 percent said that while their current plans do not include solar, they expect to include solar within five years. Only 16.9 percent said that they do not see that solar is likely to ever be competitive.

Of those who reported that they had built an active solar system, 51 percent included active, domestic water-heating systems only; 26 percent built systems for space heating and water heating only; 18 percent included solar heating for swimming pool installations; and 5 percent included a solar system for space heating, water heating, and space cooling. Of those polled in the survey, about 63 percent had not yet constructed a solar house at that time.

While emphasis in solar development initially was focused more on active systems, many builders over the years found that passive solar design can also help save energy in the homes they build.

Passive solar features seem to be the easiest for builders to incorporate into their standard building practices, although passive solar may call for some changes in design. In the 1981 *Professional Builder* study, 47.1 percent of builders carefully considered orientation of the home and window location in their home designs; 40.2 percent included a ceiling fan or power air circulator to help increase cooling effects; 11.5 percent included measures to promote natural convection in their homes; 8 percent included a greenhouse or solarium as well as landscaping and berming for passive solar benefits; and 2.3 percent included a trombe wall or water-storage wall. About 39 percent of builders polled did not include any type of passive solar design features at that time.

Some builders, it seems, are still reluctant to "go solar." In the early years of solar development, builders were often urged to proceed with caution. For many builders, it was too soon to try it, and rightly so. But building and marketing experience since then has taught valuable lessons. Some builders became discouraged. But others emerged as the solar vanguard, offering solar on a regular basis in their subdivisions, ranging from solar, domestic, water-heating systems, to active space heating, to passive solar designs.

Solar gained the credibility it needed through builder experience. The bugs were worked out of construction techniques, designs, and manufacturers' systems and warranties. And subcontractors gained in experience as qualified installers. The barriers to solar production housing are coming down.

Also, in the past, the lack of quality-control standards tended to plague the solar energy industry. Word about one bad experience with solar often created more attention than several solar successes.

To increase credibility for the industry and to help builders and consumers select reliable solar components, the Solar Energy Industries Association and the Interstate Solar Coordinating Council implemented a solar product rating. Initially only applying to solar collectors, the program required that certain specialized tests for the equipment be passed in order to qualify for a certification label. Other solar products are expected to be included as the program proceeds.

The Interstate Solar Coordinating Council is an association of thirty-eight state energy offices that recognize the certification program as assurance that solar equipment meets state solar equipment standards. Some states are expected to require certification for eligibility for tax credits or other solar incentive programs.

Solar gained credibility over the years as the solar industry developed and builders gained experience. And many solar homes were built on an individual basis, keeping architectural integrity, marketing potential, and affordability all in mind. But in the transition from construction of a single solar custom house to an entire community of attached or detached solar homes, many other aspects have to be considered. A solar development requires more coordination by the builder. While most construction techniques and design principles remain the same, the builder must also consider the impact of codes, regulations, and other ordinances that may affect his development. Certainly, codes affect the construction of one home or many. But when an entire subdivision is planned, any possible problems are intensified. It is important for builders to realize any potential difficulties before starting to plan an entire solar subdivision or even including solar as an optional feature in model homes. Fortunately, most codes or building requirements do not pose any problems.

Research reports on the HUD solar demonstration homes indicated that builders interested in solar construction should not anticipate very much interference from local building code, zoning, or tax officials. In communities where solar housing had been built, most codes were silent on solar and, in many cases, inspectors ignored the systems. When systems were reviewed, inspectors most often relied on manufacturers' descriptions and specifications. Planning, zoning, and subdivision ordinances all but ignored solar energy and its possible implications for land use regulation.

The HUD research also touched on the role of utilities. In every case studied, utility companies provided backup service at regular residential rates.

In another survey conducted by HUD, insurance companies indicated that they foresaw no major difficulties in homeowner coverage for well engineered and soundly constructed solar-energy systems. The insurance companies also indicated that for insurance purposes they did not differentiate between solar homes and those with conventional heating systems. Insurance agents reported no difficulties in obtaining policies for solar homes. Insurance rates for solar homes and conventional homes were reported about the same, according to the HUD report.

In addition, it should be noted that solar systems are not inherently impeded by building codes. Current building codes pose no major barriers to the installation of solar energy systems, according to 80 percent of local code officials in 1981. And another 64 percent of these officials indicated that they foresaw no future problems with the acceptance of solar systems and design.

These results were derived from a 1981 survey of local code officials by HUD and the Department of Energy. Data were based on the analysis of building regulatory information gathered during HUD's solar demonstration program in the late 1970s. The survey was conducted to determine whether building code officials were unnecessarily rejecting solar projects because building codes did not address these systems.

The technical issues of incorporating solar systems into building designs were studied by a portion of code departments. About 25 percent of local building code officials said that their departments had investigated the potential impact of solar energy on building codes. Among these departments, about one-third indicated that standards were needed for solar systems and components. And about 19 percent said that their codes already included provisions for solar systems.

At the time of the survey and report, solar buildings faced no greater problems in gaining approval than non-solar buildings. But about 21 percent of local building code officials indicated that it took longer to process a solar project than a standard, conventional building. The officials also indicated that design changes had to be made in about 20 percent of the systems, not directly related to the solar system, but to structural and ventilation problems. Most officials reported that additional site inspections were needed for solar-system installations.

The outlook for the acceptance of solar-energy systems looks bright among these officials. Among those interviewed, about one-half of the building code officials said that their local codes encourage energy conservation. About 41 percent said that an energy conservation program within the city or county government was promoted among builders. Officials also indicated the need for educational materials to aid them in evaluating equipment and design and in making decisions about solar-system installations in residential development.

A builder should cooperate in helping familiarize these officials with the nuts-and-bolts of solar. A well-designed and informative presentation to officials could help open many doors and prevent any delays in the approval process for a solar development.

But while code officials tend to look favorably on solar homes, builders need to keep certain requirements in mind. Passive solar components, for instance, incorporated into a building's structure should comply with codes applying to structural building materials, according to guidelines for building code officials from the Department of Energy.

The guidelines recommend that a passive solar component that also serves a structural function in the building should be treated first as a structural building material, rather than primarily as part of an energy system. Most of these structural elements will be installed by the same subcontractor whether the component serves as a passive solar element or just a structural member, the guidelines stated. Building components, particularly in passive solar homes, often function in a dual role in the building's structure and in the home's energy system.

Another important legal aspect in building a solar development or community is solar access rights. A builder must make sure that one building does not shade a neighboring house or unit, particularly in higher density developments. These are called solar access rights. It is one thing to maximize solar exposure for one home, but the same "right to the sun's rays" needs to be assured to neighbors as well.

Careful site planning and landscaping are necessities for builders to prevent these problems. But solar access rights may also require the estab-

lishment of a neighborhood covenant to prevent future construction of other buildings and structures or planting of vegetation such as tall trees which may block a neighbor's access to solar rays. These covenants protect the homeowners' rights and a builder's reputation for future solar developments. In some localities, zoning ordinances require establishment of solar access rights in a solar development.

While some codes and zoning ordinances are slowly changing to *protect* use of solar energy in developments, other ordinances are being developed to *promote* use of solar energy in entire communities.

In some areas of the country, solar is required to some extent in all new construction by an ordinance. Solar is not an option for a builder. It is a *requirement* for residential development as part of a municipal or county building code or energy-conservation policy.

Many cities have recognized the potential impact of solar by developing progressive energy policies in their communities. One of the first major ordinances of this kind was passed in San Diego, California. The local ordinance required that solar water-heating systems be installed in all new construction in unincorporated areas of San Diego County. Unincorporated areas not served by natural pipeline gas were required to begin using solar water heaters as of October 1, 1979. And after October 1, 1980, all new construction in unincorporated areas was required to include solar water heating. The ordinance stated various energy goals which culminated in one basic objective: to achieve maximum conservation practices and maximum development of renewable alternative sources of energy.

Many other communities have followed suit with similar regulations on new construction. Some take the form of an incentive, rather than a requirement. In Lincoln, Nebraska, for instance, a builder can receive a 20 percent increase in unit density by voluntarily protecting solar access through use of protective covenants and appropriate preplanning.

Other ordinances and incentives abound in cities and counties across the United States. They have encouraged development of solar in their respective jurisdictions, but they have also promoted use of solar in surrounding unrestricted areas where these ordinances could possibly be established in the next few years. An entire solar development requires some preplanning, whether the homes incorporate active or passive solar systems. Many builders want to stay one step ahead of the game. They do not want their projects on the drawing board today to become obsolete before they are in the ground tomorrow.

But builders are also realizing that market demand for energy efficiency is leading to an increase in the perceived value of solar homes by buyers. Energy efficiency is an important consideration among buyers of production housing. Active and passive solar are being recognized more and more as an important part of potential energy savings.

For most builders, their first solar construction experience in building a solar home or development is visibly on the horizon and getting closer. But other builders, comparably, are already reaping the rewards.

Planning for a Large-Scale Solar Development

The marketing of solar energy emerged as a major housing trend of the 1980s. Anticipating greater demand and requirements for energy efficiency, builders began incorporating solar features into their housing developments.

In 1980, *Professional Builder* magazine asked California architect Barry Berkus to conceive a prototype for a large-scale project that would demonstrate passive solar design in production housing. Simultaneously, Berkus was starting to plan a 663-attached-unit passive solar community for the Christiana Companies of San Diego, California. Christiana, at the vanguard of the trend, had initiated a solar task force to investigate the viability of including solar-energy elements into its future housing projects.

Their research and planning led to the formulation of the Villa Corte development. Construction of the project was scheduled to begin in September 1981.

Villa Corte incorporated practical passive solar ideas in a common housing product, said solar consultant J. Randall Roberts of Irvine, California, who was involved in the development of the plans. A hybrid solar system was designed to combine passive solar design with active solar technology and a conventional backup heating and cooling system. "Villa Corte will be a testing ground for Christiana," Roberts said, "to enable them to study a solar development from scratch and monitor the finished product."

Designed by Berkus Group Architects of Santa Barbara, California, the project combined high-density attached housing with energy-efficient solar design. Villa Corte specifically was designed to overcome difficulties associated with production solar housing, such as solar access and orientation of every unit to a southern exposure.

The cross-section drawing (pages 168–169) details how units were arranged to maximize natural heating and cooling. Solar components included:

- A south-facing attached greenhouse in all units;
- Cross circulation through operable windows, skylights, clerestory windows, and ceiling fans;
- Thermal mass in the form of a concrete floor to absorb passive solar heat gain;
- Double-glazed windows;
- Insulating curtains for glazing areas with an R value of 15 or more, operated manually or by electricity;
- Exterior wall insulation of R11 to R19 with common walls insulated to R22;
- Ceilings insulated to a minimum of R19.

To maximize passive solar heat gain from the southern exposure, two types of units were designed. Three of the model floor plans were oriented to views of the greenbelt area. Primary living areas were located in the front of these plans. Three other models provided views of a private courtyard with living areas focused to the rear of the units. Entrances to all units were located along the greenbelts.

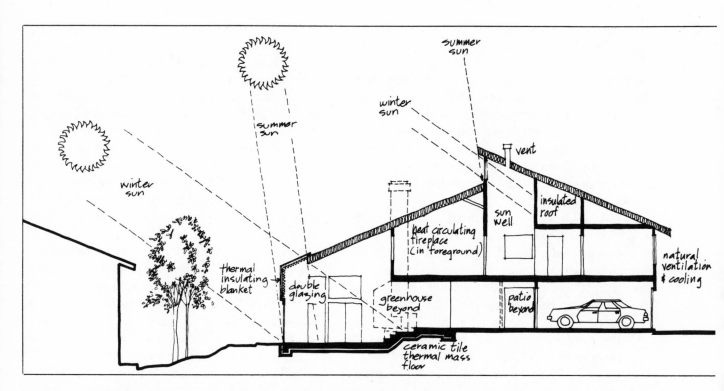

The cross-sectional drawing shows how the passive solar system works and how the buildings are related by a common access lane. The project was designed by Berkus Group Architects and developed by Christiana Companies.

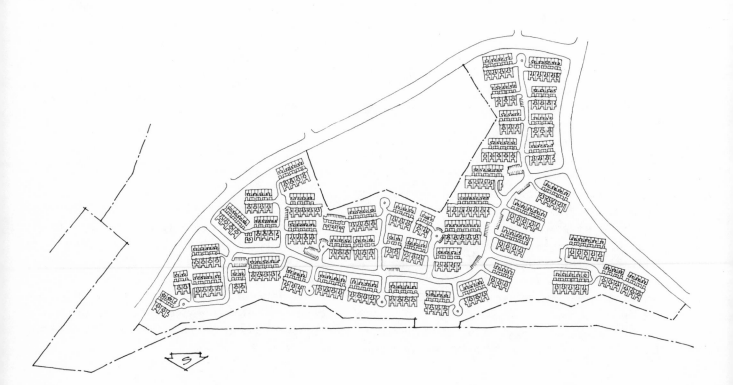

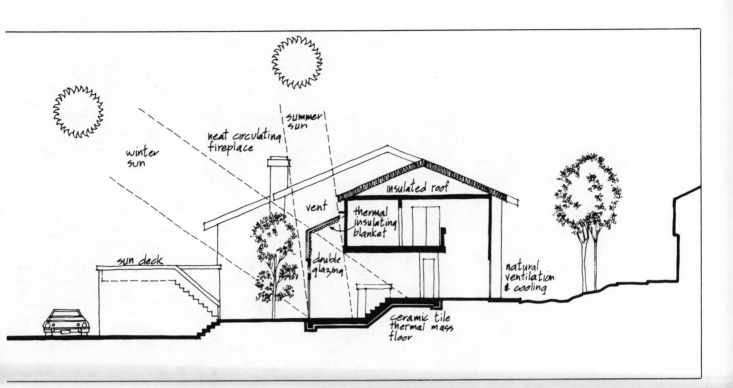

Villa Corte was a planned solar community of 663 attached units in San Diego, California. The site plan, at left, shows how all of the units are oriented to the south for passive solar heat gain with a density of ten units per acre. Two types of units were designed for solar orientation.

deck sitting

gar

mbr #2

hobby

d

mbr #1

greenhouse
below

open

K

bar

nook

dr

60" high
shelf

lv

2nd FLOOR

1st FLOOR

For optimal solar orientation, two basic units were designed
for Villa Corte. Plans and elevational drawings of the first
prototypes reveal living areas placed at the front of the units
facing a greenbelt. Entrances of these units were located on
the southern exposure. All units in the planned community
include rear-loading garages.

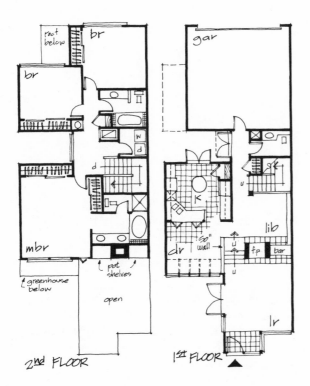

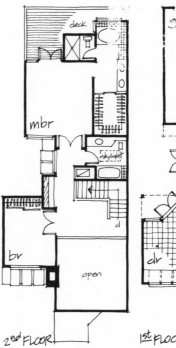

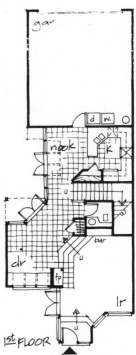

2ⁿᵈ FLOOR

1ˢᵗ FLOOR

2ⁿᵈ FLOOR

1ˢᵗ FLOOR

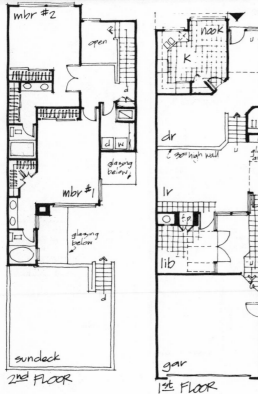

mbr #2

open

d w

glazing
below

mbr #1

glazing
below

sundeck

2ⁿᵈ FLOOR

nook

K

dr

~30" high wall

bar

glass
above

lv

fp

lib

gar

1ˢᵗ FLOOR

The second type of unit at Villa Corte was designed to focus living areas around a rear courtyard. Courtyards and garages face south. Entrances face north to a greenbelt. The elevational drawing shows rear views from the common access lane between buildings.

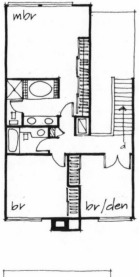

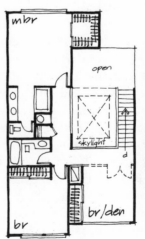

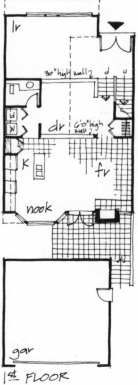

mbr

nook

br

br/den

K

dr

lr

f.p.

bar

gar

2nd FLOOR

1st FLOOR

mbr

open

skylight

br

br/den

lr

30" high wall

dr

K

fr

nook

gar

2nd FLOOR

1st FLOOR

S

About 75 percent of glazing in the units was oriented to the southern exposure for passive solar heat gain. A minimal amount of glass was located on the north side of each unit.

To adapt the plans to northern climates, Berkus suggested that windows on the north side of the unit be reduced even further in size and a vestibule entry be added to minimize heat loss.

Floor plans incorporated both energy and lifestyle considerations. Within the units, passive solar heating and cooling was aided by the open interior plans. Multiple levels, rather than restricting walls, define spaces. Living areas were focused to the greenbelt or courtyard, depending on unit type and solar orientation.

Garages were rear-loading with access from a common lane between buildings. The lane and low garages provided a sense of privacy and separation from the other buildings, Berkus noted. But at the same time, the lanes prevented units from being shaded by neighboring buildings. Solar access is an important element to consider in designing production solar housing. Units and landscaping must be arranged to minimize shadowing on southern exposures.

Passive solar required a rigid site plan (shown on page 170), said architect Berkus. Streets at Villa Corte were planned to run east to west to maximize solar orientation. But the major artery was curved to provide visual interest from the street. Buildings of four to ten attached units were sited with a variance of 45 degrees from due south.

For market flexibility, the units were designed basically as seventy foot by twenty-five foot modules. The makeup of units in each building could be interchanged without affecting the site plan. A density of ten units per acre was achieved.

A centralized, active solar water-heating system was also planned. Such a system was less expensive and more efficient to operate and install than individual systems, Roberts said. Active solar hardware and mechanical systems were located in remote arrays in the greenbelt areas. Because the active solar equipment was not tied to the architecture, the system can be changed and updated as needed. "The state of the art is changing continually," Berkus noted. "And we want to avoid antiquation."

Christiana's management expects that many builders soon could be caught with an outmoded, non-solar housing product. Not unlike the American automobile industry, builders might be offering a product that is unresponsive to the market demand for energy efficiency. "Solar will move to the forefront of housing in the not-so-distant future," said Frank Ferdon, vice-president of sales and marketing for Christiana and a member of the firm's solar task force. "We want to make provisions for solar now in the original designs of our future housing products."

The Christiana solar task force brought together mid-to-upper management executives from every major division within the company, including sales and marketing, engineering, finance, design, acquisitions, and legal areas. The task force and its consultants examined existing solar systems and products as well as new technology for the development of Villa Corte and other future developments. Cost efficiency was one of the major considerations.

Christiana has continued to explore the feasibility of including other passive and active solar features at the Villa Corte project.

The solar industry is basically new and unproven in terms of mass production, Ferdon noted. For a community developer with large-scale projects, one of the major obstacles was the lack of a long-term solar project with a track record. But Berkus pointed out that the future of solar in production housing is very bright, and the technology is not limited to high-priced, custom, detached housing.

"There is a common language between custom and production housing with solar," he said. Solar principles are the same for both types of housing.

And in the 80s, theory will become common practice.

Solar Subdivision Can Make A Marketing Difference

A combination of passive and active solar features can make a significant difference in the cost of operating homes . . . and in marketing them, says builder John Mourier of Roseville, California. "Point out the economical advantages to buyers."

"People are looking at how much it costs to live in a house. Their way of thinking is changing," he noted.

Using a radiant slab system with active solar collectors and passive solar design and landscaping, the thirty-five houses in Mourier's Sunpointe solar subdivision in suburban Sacramento were designed to achieve about 83 percent efficiency on space heating and cooling as well as domestic water heating. (Using passive solar design alone, the houses rated a 69 percent efficiency on space heating.)

These energy savings provided a marketing plus. Utility bills in 1981 were estimated at about $11 per month, compared to $50 to $75 per month for a similarly sized home which uses a conventional gas-fired system or heat pump.

But savings on utility bills are only the beginning. Mourier also pointed out to buyers the other economical advantages of buying a solar home. The Federal Housing Authority allows a higher

loan-to-value to compensate for the cost of the solar system. The solar houses also qualify for a 40 percent federal tax credit on the cost of the $8000 Trident solar system. State solar tax credits can also be taken. Mourier noted in comparison that there are no tax credits for the cost of installing a conventional HVAC system.

In Mourier's homes, the cost of a conventional furnace system was eliminated in the homes, further bringing down the net cost of the solar system. Backup heating and cooling are inherent in the solar system through use of in-line strip heaters and chillers.

Additional savings for buyers was achieved from Pacific Gas and Electric's Suntherm program which awarded $1000 bonus per home, based on the homes' efficiency levels. These savings were passed on to the buyer.

Ranging in price from $79,000 to $89,000 in 1981, the 1300- to 1500-square-foot, detached homes compared competitively with others in price. But there was no comparison in traffic. Mourier's houses drew about one hundred and fifty

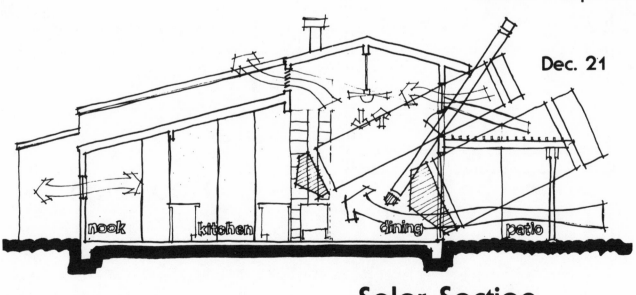

Mar. 21 - Sept. 21

Dec. 21

Solar Section

The solar system in the Sunpointe homes in suburban Sacramento was based on passive solar design and an active solar system. A cross-section of the passive solar design shows how passive solar heat gain is maximized in winter months and minimized in summer months.

Floor Plan

The Sunpointe floor plan shows how rooms were oriented so that living areas can take advantage of passive solar heat gain. The active solar heating and cooling system is based on a radiant slab concept. The schematic drawing, right, demonstrates how water is circulated throughout the solar collectors and slab. (See also photo on page 161.)

Solar
collectors

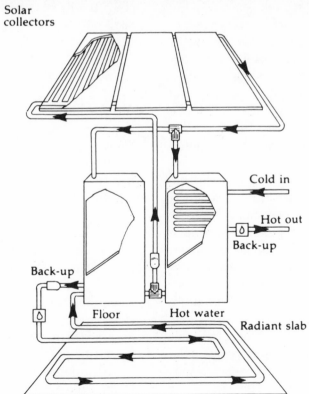

Cold in

Hot out

Back-up

Back-up

Floor

Hot water

Radiant slab

visitors per weekend, compared with other models in the area which attracted about five. "And there were a lot of very serious buyers," Mourier said. He was surprised to find energy efficiency high in the priorities of homebuyers. "I thought it was only a secondary consideration," he said. "I was surprised." In the first six weeks, seven units were sold.

"We emphasized the actual dollars that homeowners would save," Mourier said. "A solar home will appreciate faster due to lower operating costs." And the tax credits help offset the cost of the initial additional investment.

Mourier held a seminar for about 120 area realtors on solar homes and how they work. It was designed to educate them and train the sales staff. The seminar resulted in no direct sales initially from realtors, "but it gave us a lot of good exposure," Mourier said.

In addition to an extra marketing effort with the local realtors, Mourier noted that it took a little more time in initially planning a solar subdivision than a conventional one. For instance, the streets should run east and west whenever possible to provide the greatest number of lots with north and south exposures.

He also pointed out that solar access needs to be kept in consideration. This will affect the placement of the house on the lot and careful landscaping to avoid shading neighboring houses. He drew up a written covenant within the community of homes to prevent any future problems with solar access. He noted that local governments are becoming more active in promoting energy conservation.

Mourier designed the houses so that the majority of glazing is south-facing. Either side of the house can serve as the front elevation. The only difference is that the garages flip-flop to accommodate these changes and provide access to the street. All three plans, then, can be used on any lot without customized changes. For those units with east or west orientation, the glazing is oriented towards the south and the roof line changes.

Inside the houses, Mourier found favorable buyer response to the open feeling of passive solar design. In the whole house, there are only basically three doors—for the bedrooms. The rest of the living space is open for maximum natural air circulation.

Energy-saving features included: R11 wall and R30 ceiling insulation, slab insulation, double-glazed windows, wood stove, active solar radiant heating and cooling, active solar water heating, passive solar design, trellises to eliminate solar gain through glazed areas in the summer, and a roof turbine commonly used in non-residential buildings to exhaust hot interior air and draw in cool evening breezes.

In actual figures, the passive and active solar features added about 20 percent to raw construction costs. For example, the hard construction costs for one of his models, without land, was about $36,700. About $6,700 of those costs were incurred from the inclusion of the passive and active solar features.

In the construction of his first solar subdivision, Mourier found that a little extra time and effort were needed. "It was not as conventional as tract housing," he said, pointing to the fact that it was his first attempt at solar. "Anything new needs more coordination." But despite the extra work, Mourier said that the majority of his houses from now on will be solar. "The market is there," he said.

A Solar House Built from Standard Plans

Many active and passive solar houses have been designed from scratch. But many builders overlook standard plans that may be readily adaptable to accommodating active solar hardware or oriented to take advantage of passive solar techniques.

Taking the lead with many other builders, Alpha Construction Co. Inc. of Canton, Ohio, incorporated solar panels on standard house designs in 1977. Granted four awards through the solar grant program conducted by the Department of Housing and Urban Development, the firm varied house plans, roof pitches, siting, and type of houses for testing purposes. One of the models was built directly from a standard Plan of the Month featured in the February 1977 issue of *Professional Builder*.

A 1863-square-foot, active solar house was built from a non-solar Professional Builder *Plan of the Month featured in Febru-ary 1977. The chimney-like structure between the house and garage (shown in the photo on the rear elevation) contained the ductwork carrying heated air from the panels to the storage system.*

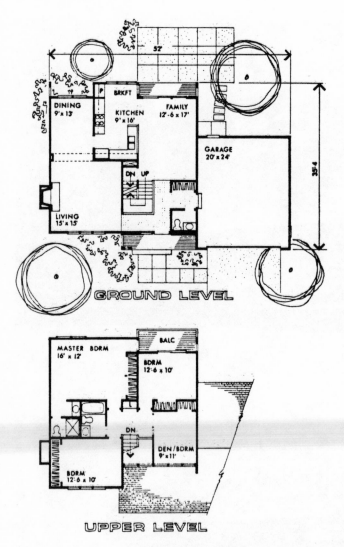

GROUND LEVEL

UPPER LEVEL

The floor plan features 958 square feet on the main level and 905 square feet on the upper level. The 32-foot foundation can take a one or two-car garage, depending on the site and cost factors.

Designed by architect John D. Bloodgood A.I.A. of Des Moines, Iowa, the Plan of the Month did not specify solar. But the builder found that he could add active solar hardware to the house exactly as shown on the plans. The roof pitch provided an adequate angle for solar collection in his region of the country. An air-type active solar collection system was installed in the $79,900 house in late 1977. The manufacturer, Solar Energy Products of Avon Lake, Ohio, estimated that the system would supply about 50 percent of the heat and 70 percent of the hot water for the house. But actual monitored savings on space heat only reached 35 percent to 48 percent in the winter months.

The $35,600 grant allowed about $7,500 to $10,000 per house for installation of active solar heat and water heating on four houses.

A small builder of about thirty to thirty-five houses per year, Alpha found that 4000 people passed through the houses when they were open as models in late 1977. The four houses sold between $68,800 and $79,900.

"Alpha believes in energy-efficient homes, solar or not," said Ron Braucher, secretary/treasurer of the firm. In keeping with the firm's insulation standards, the solar houses were built identical to standard models with R17 to R20 wall insulation and R36 ceiling insulation. "It costs more," Braucher said, "but it pays off."

Alpha also completed two houses with "solar potential." Proper siting and roof pitch were considered and ductwork was installed for future active solar hardware. "Someday costs will justify active solar," Braucher said. "We can't sell (active) solar now because of the still low costs of energy in our area." He estimated gas heat and electricity at only about $72 per month in 1980.

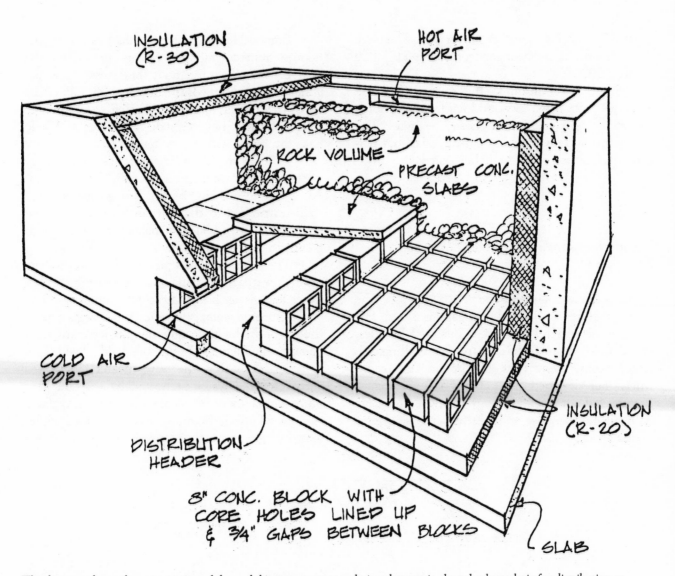

INSULATION
(R-30)

HOT AIR
PORT

ROCK VOLUME

PRECAST CONC.
SLABS

COLD AIR
PORT

INSULATION
(R-20)

DISTRIBUTION
HEADER

8" CONC. BLOCK WITH
CORE HOLES LINED UP
& 3/4" GAPS BETWEEN BLOCKS

SLAB

The diagram shows the construction of the rock bin storage system designed to retain the solar heated air for distribution as space heat and hot water. It was designed by Solar Energy Products of Avon Lake, Ohio.

Located in an area where many people are skeptical about the viability of solar energy, "the data collected from the HUD houses will help answer questions about cost efficiency," Braucher said. The time for active solar economics there has not yet arrived.

One lesson that Alpha learned from constructing the houses was that while an active solar hot-air system was good for space heat, a liquid-type system would be more efficient for active solar water heating, considering the cost of electricity to circulate the hot air to produce hot water, he said.

Alpha planned on using the hard facts about solar from the HUD houses as a marketing tool. "Solar is a step in the right direction with a good house value for the future," Braucher said.

Active solar is still part of the future, as far as Alpha is concerned. Alpha constructed one active solar house originally and four others with the HUD grant. But since 1978 and the grant program, the firm has not constructed any more active solar houses. But Alpha moved ahead with other alternative ways of heating a house. By 1980, 45 percent of the homes that Alpha built were "heavily oriented to passive solar," Braucher said. The price of the houses in 1980 ranged from about $105,000 to $260,000.

Proper orientation to the south with more windows on that exposure and fewer on the north provided no real additional costs, he said. "The homes are not advertised as passive solar, but it is certainly pointed out," Braucher noted.

Plenum Heat/Solar Hot Water Saves 60 to 75 Percent

In many homes claimed to be "energy saving," the energy features are merely stop-gap measures. The basic house remains the same. But Fred Brandes, president of Brandes & Roy Inc. of Wallingford, Connecticut, went back to the drawing board when he designed his energy-saving homes. Brandes did not just add energy-saving features. He built his model house around them into an energy saving *system*.

Brandes' heating system is ductless, using the floor plenums for radiant heat and circulating the heat continually throughout the house. (See diagram.) Blowers run continually at about half of the speed of a typical forced-air heating system. Three solar collectors help provide hot water and help heat the house with the water heater.

"We use the hot water heater as the boiler by circulating hot water through a coil," Brandes said. Air is heated by being blown through the coil and then distributed to the plenum floors on the first and second stories. Heat radiates through the floor boards to heat the house.

The solar collectors preheat the water for the oil-fired water heater, making the heating and hot water load easier on the heating equipment. "The solar-tempered water saves energy and helps extend the life of the heating equipment by lessening temperature fluctuations," Brandes said. Instead of heating cold water, the water heater is supplied with tempered water preheated by the sun to a minimum of about 90 degrees on most sunny days.

In addition, Brandes' system included triple-glazed windows; weather-stripped steel entry doors;

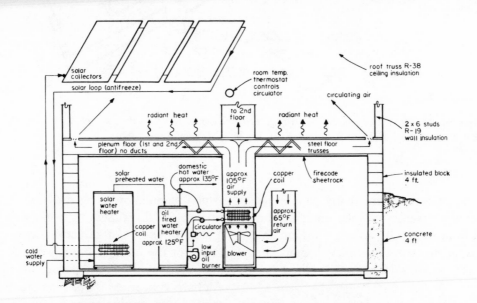

The Brandes energy building system incorporated solar collectors to preheat water for the water heater. In addition, the water heater acts as the home's boiler by circulating hot water through a copper coil. Air is blown through the coil up into the plenum floors. Using no ducts, the floors act as radiant heaters.

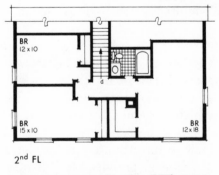

2nd FL

BR
12 x 10

BR
15 x 10

BR
12 x 18

BR
12 x 11

K

LR
20 x 11

DR
12 x 11

1st FL

Brandes' solar saltbox model combined the benefits of active and passive solar energy features. The three copper solar collectors help provide hot water and heat for the house. The saltbox design helps protect the house against the bitter winter winds. PHOTOS: Duszak Studio.

183

R19-insulated exterior walls (six inches of glass fiber); R38-insulated ceiling (twelve inches of glass fiber); and insulated concrete block in the basement.

In a northeastern climate with an October to May heating season (6000 annual degree days), the system was estimated to save about 60 to 75 percent on annual heating and hot water costs, compared with a similar, tract-built, four-bedroom house with standard R11 wall and R19 ceiling insulation.

Brandes pointed out that those savings could mean about $600 to $700 per year savings on an average. Payback for the $4000 cost of the energy system at 1979 oil prices (about 50 cents per gallon) was estimated at five to six years. Increased oil prices would lower the estimated payback period.

For a family of four, estimated annual costs for heat and hot water, using an estimated 500 gallons of oil at 50 cents per gallon, would cost the owner about $250 per year. In the period from May 1978 to mid-November 1978, the 1728-square-foot, Brandes model home ran up a heating and hot water bill of $46.50, using 93 gallons of oil, under simulated living conditions. (About 70 gallons of hot water at 132 degrees Fahrenheit was dumped every day to simulate family use.)

Metering equipment was expected to be installed in the model later to calculate exact data with actual living conditions, under the direction of the Northeast Solar Energy Center in Boston, Massachusetts. The center also analyzed other collected data. With the exception of the metering equipment, Brandes did not receive any government funds or subsidies to develop or build his solar model house.

Brandes' model home design reached back about 200 years to traditional New England saltbox architecture—to what Brandes called an original passive solar house. The saltbox house was originally oriented towards the sun with most of the window openings facing south for heat gain. On the north side of the house, the long sloping roof helped protect the house from bitter winter winds. (See photos on page 183.)

The estimated cost of the Brandes solar saltbox model, excluding land, septic, and landscaping, was about $48,700 in January 1979, including the $4,000 energy system. The basic heating system, including solar, cost about $2,500 to $3,000. Added insulation cost about $500, and upgraded windows added about $500.

Brandes noted that of the three major components of his system, the added insulation and insulated doors and windows contribute the most energy savings. The plenum distribution method adds the next largest share of savings. And the solar collectors supplement the insulation and plenum distribution.

The size of the solar system installed on a Brandes home, typically three copper solar collectors and an 80-gallon tank, depends on the size of the homeowner's family. The solar system also was designed to adapt to new developments in solar energy in the future, allowing the owner to add more collectors and a larger storage tank.

With patents pending on his system, Brandes licensed other builders in his area to incorporate his energy system in their home designs. Brandes has concentrated his efforts through franchised builders.

In January 1979, twelve of the homes using Brandes' energy system were under construction, ranging in sales price from $50,000 to $150,000.

Sell a Community with Solar "Potential"

For most builders, a solar-heated model house is almost a guarantee of opening-day crowds and big traffic figures. But while most buyers will come out to look, many won't touch a solar house because of currently high up-front costs and the real or imagined problems with solar energy systems. The question is: How to turn the lookers into buyers.

Sam Primack, president of Perl Mack Corp. of Denver, solved the problem for himself by building homes with *solar potential*. In early 1977, Primack began volume production of single-family, three-bedroom homes designed to use solar heating initially, or convert whenever the owner wished to do so. With increasing gas rates, decreasing gas availability, and more than 300 sunny days per year in the Denver area, the outlook for solar energy was bright.

Production line shows Primack's initial twenty-two solar houses under construction in Denver in early 1977. All were sold in one weekend. All houses in the community were built to be capable of converting to solar energy. PHOTO: Robert W. Schott.

To kick off the development, Primack actually installed solar heating and hot water systems into twenty-two homes in the community at no additional cost to the buyer. He covered the cost of the solar installations with a grant of $9000 per home through the residential solar heating demonstration program conducted by the Department of Housing and Urban Development. All twenty-two houses were sold the first day on the market.

Although the other houses in the community, which ranged in price from $46,900 to $49,900 in 1977, did not provide solar heating, they contained the basics for *solar conversion*. An 800-gallon concrete storage tank was placed in every house when the foundation was laid. The houses' conventional gas-heating furnaces were designed for retrofit when a solar system was installed. Also, the houses required no structural alterations to accommodate a solar system. The roof pitch was angled for the best exposure to the sun. The roof was also constructed to take the added weight of the collectors. Piping and ductwork were completed in the finished portion of the house for later conversion or initial installation. The houses were also sited on the lots to provide the maximum exposure to the sun and protect the homeowner from a neighbor's shade.

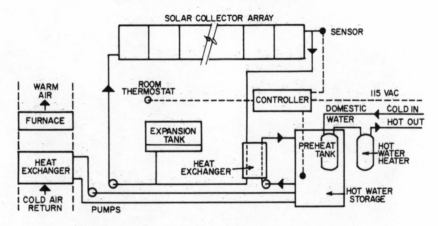

PRIMACK'S SOLAR HEATING SYSTEM

The diagram illustrates Primack's hydronic solar system. The solar heating system was designed to save up to 70 percent of heating and hot-water requirements. If the thermostat temperature was not met by solar energy, the gas-fired, forced-air furnace would automatically operate until the desired temperature was reached.

Step-by-Step Solar

1. An 800-gallon concrete storage tank, piping, and ducts were installed in every house for future conversion to solar.

2. A high-lift loader brought 18 to 20 solar panels to the roofs for installation. The panels weighed about 200 pounds.

3. Workers placed panels on the roof, caulking around the edges and pipes to insulate and prevent leaks.

4. Roofers applied ordinary shingles or shakes to the remainder of the roof after the solar panels were installed. PHOTOS: Robert W. Schott.

One of Primack's three model houses showed that, yes, solar houses can have curb appeal. PHOTO: Robert W. Schott.

The houses also included energy conservation features.

"We're making sure that the house we're building today," Primack said, "is not going to be part of the energy problem in the years to come."

Design an Entire Passive Solar Development

A solar house is a better investment than a conventional home, according to 86 percent of prospective buyers who toured builder Patrick Bowe's passive solar model house in Richmond, Virginia. And 96 percent said that they like the concept of passive solar energy.

The model was located in Bowe's 213-unit passive solar development of single-family detached homes which opened in June 1980. Ten available passive solar plans were priced from $65,000 to $80,000.

Buyers are burdened by high interest rates and high monthly heating bills, said Bowe, president of Century 21/Virginia Homes Unlimited in Richmond.

But those problems give a marketing edge to Bowe's passive solar development. An advertisement attracted "literally thousands of people who are all interested in solar," said Bowe. About 40 percent of those who toured the model were actively seeking to purchase a house. In the first three months, eleven passive solar units were sold.

Based on heat loss calculations made in the spring of 1980, the passive solar houses would cost about $240 per year to heat and $228 to cool, according to the local utility company. But Bowe notes that the utility did not at that time take heat *gain* into consideration. At the same time, an independent computer analysis estimated that it would cost less than $100 per year to heat the homes.

The utility company estimated that an additional 25 percent could be saved on the heating bill if moveable insulation was used over glazed areas at

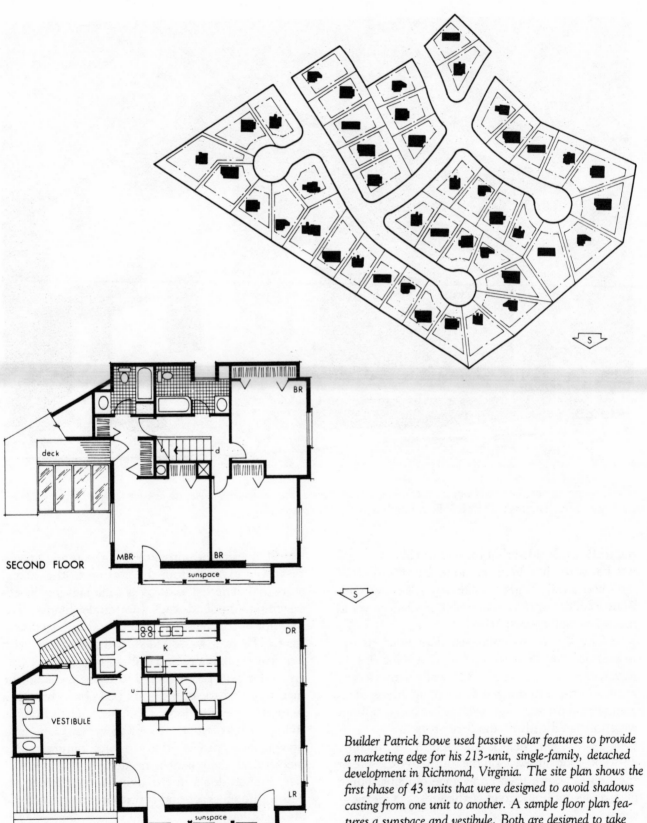

SECOND FLOOR

FIRST FLOOR

Builder Patrick Bowe used passive solar features to provide a marketing edge for his 213-unit, single-family, detached development in Richmond, Virginia. The site plan shows the first phase of 43 units that were designed to avoid shadows casting from one unit to another. A sample floor plan features a sunspace and vestibule. Both are designed to take advantage of passive solar heat gain.

The southern exposure of one of Bowe's exterior model elevations is shown above. All elevations were designed for any side of the house to face the street. PHOTO: Don Eiler's Custom Photography.

night. Bowe decided that the additional cost would not be worth it. "With an annual heating bill of less than $100, it just wouldn't pay," Bowe said. "The $2000 cost of the moveable insulation would mean an eighty-year payback."

The key to an energy-efficient house is the insulation, said Bowe. An insulative value of R22 was achieved by covering R11-walls with Dryvit, an insulating exterior material commonly used in commercial projects. Using fiberglass batts, ceilings were insulated to R30 and floors to R13.

Passive solar heat is collected in a 30-inch by 24-to-30-foot sunspace on the southern exposure of the houses. Bowe used an average of eight sliding glass doors per house to glaze the sunspace inexpensively.

Between the sunspace and the living area, a mass wall extends from the footing to the second story roof. The wall consists of solar masonry blocks weighing 80 pounds each (not cinder block). The exterior of this mass wall was dyed black to absorb heat. The wall was divided into two stories with vents along the floor and ceiling of each story. Passive solar heat is distributed to living areas on the first floor and to second-story bedrooms through a natural convection loop. Heated air moves into the living areas through the ceiling vents. Cool air is drawn back through the sunspace naturally. No mechanical equipment is needed.

French doors in the living room provide access to the sunspace and contribute to natural light and ventilation.

In summer, the vents can be closed and sliding glass doors in the sunspace opened to prevent heat build-up. The second floor of the sunspace provides an overhang to shade the first floor from the summer sun.

A vestibule also contributes passive solar heat by acting as a greenhouse. The room is enclosed by sliding glass doors and three-foot by six-foot glass panels on the roof of the southern exposure.

Bowe estimated that less than 5 percent of the cost of the house was attributed to passive solar components including the mass wall, extra glazing, overhang, and a masonry tile floor covering in the greenhouse area.

To orient the houses toward the sun, elevations were designed for any view of the house to face the street. The site plan was designed to avoid houses shading each other. Shadows were figured for December 21, the shortest day of the year when shadows are the longest.

To refine his initial marketing approach to focus on more serious buyers, Bowe redesigned his advertising to draw fewer curiosity seekers. The new advertisement played "more on a liveable house with a liveable heating bill," Bowe said.

And in times when buyers are concerned about the high monthly cost of housing, "that is where we come ahead."

Produce a Standard Model

Until the 1980s, most passive (and active) solar houses were custom designs on scattered sites. But a number of innovative builders, like M. J. Brock & Sons in Sacramento, California, proved that passive solar principles were easily adaptable in production housing. The passive solar techniques use the home's actual structure to heat and cool the

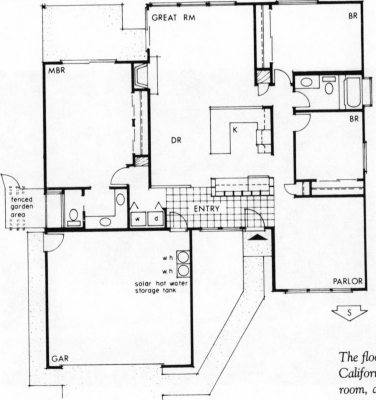

The floor plan for the Brock Sundial model in Sacramento, California, included several passive solar features. The great room, dining area, and kitchen are open to the entry to maximize passive solar heating and air circulation.

house, rather than using mechanical equipment such as active solar collectors.

In the spring of 1980, Brock began offering a 1616-square-foot, passive solar house along with its other models. Selling then for about $80,000, the three-bedroom/two-bath Sundial plan was constructed for about $49.50 per square foot, including land.

Passive solar construction added about $1 per square foot to the cost of the house, said marketing manager Steve Brock. Passive solar features included south-facing windows, a solar mass wall (to absorb the sun's heat in winter and cool evening air in summer), double-glazed windows, R30 ceiling insulation, R11 wall insulation, perimeter insulation, and a ceiling fan. The units also included active solar water heating and an energy-efficient fireplace with a heat exchanger.

But the list of features does not tell the whole story. About three years prior to the development of the passive solar model, the firm began orienting its streets east and west. This orientation provided 80 percent of the lots with north and south expo-sures, allowing the sun to help heat the house naturally through south-facing windows.

The passive solar model was the next step in energy-efficient housing, said Steve Brock. Computer simulations estimated that the passive solar features would help save about 50 to 60 percent on the home's heating bill. It should be noted that actual savings from any energy-efficient house will depend on the lifestyle of the owner.

Brock admitted that the house took a little more time than usual to design and plan, but the actual construction was very typical.

One interesting feature of the house was the solar mass wall which was constructed of 120 square feet of jumbo slumpstone block, grout filled. The total cost for the mass wall was about $600, or $5 per square foot.

The wall was disguised as a partition dividing the kitchen from the entry. But while it looked like just a decorative brick wall, the wall was designed to absorb the sun's heat through large glass areas in the entry. An exposed concrete slab floor in the entry also helped absorb excess heat. In winter

The Brock passive solar model was designed for both energy efficiency and for marketability. The 1616-square-foot model house sold for about $80,000 in mid-1980. Note that the large glass areas in the entry capture rays from the low winter sun.

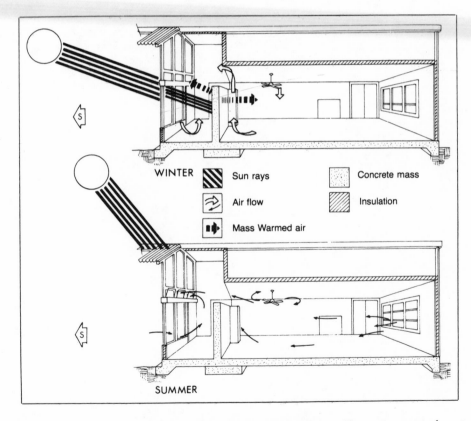

WINTER

▨	Sun rays	▦	Concrete mass
↻	Air flow	▨	Insulation
◼▶	Mass Warmed air		

SUMMER

The living area of the Sundial model was open to aid circulation of heat in winter and cool air in summer. The brick wall that separates the kitchen and the tile entry floor were both designed to absorb the sun to help heat the house in the winter months. The ceiling fan recirculates the air.

months, the heat absorbed by the wall is transmitted into the room. As the heat rises, the air is recirculated by the ceiling fan. The interior design of the living area is open to aid circulation.

In summer, an overhang and trellis over the entry help block out the sun which is at a much higher angle in those months. The mass wall absorbs cool night air to modulate daytime temperatures inside the house. The ceiling fan also keeps the cool air circulating.

Brock pointed out that although the plan was designed to provide substantial energy savings, the house does not look unusual. In fact, it was a marketable model. Brock considered the plan to be one of their best, independent of the passive solar features. By the end of 1980, ten passive solar units had been sold.

As a promotion tool, one passive solar home was given away in a drawing. To acquaint the public with passive solar features in the model, people were required to drop off the entry form at one of the Brock sales centers.

About 30 percent of the units in the subdivision will incorporate the Sundial design. Out of the four models offered at this project, only one was passive solar. But Brock's plans included two new subdivisions which offer only passive solar models. The subdivisions began sales in the spring of 1981.

Brock considers passive solar the "leading edge in new technology." An increasing number of houses in the next few years are expected to incorporate passive solar construction. It is the wave of the future, utilizing the world's oldest and most sensible heating source—the sun.

APPENDIX

For More Solar Information. . . .

Much additional information and assistance on solar energy is available from many sources, ranging from free publications on building and selling solar homes to technical assistance provided by qualified staff. Many sources even have listings of local builders and installers who are well versed in solar construction.

The federal government is, perhaps, the largest single source of information on solar energy through several agencies and departments. The primary federal agency that handles requests for information on solar energy is the national solar heating and cooling information center which is called the *Conservation and Renewable Energy Inquiry and Referral Service*. The office will answer general requests for information and can provide numerous publications on solar energy, including solar construction and marketing for builders. Technical questions are referred to other agencies or industry sources.

The mailing address is: *Renewable Energy Information*, P.O. Box 8900, Silver Spring, Maryland 20907. Toll-free phone numbers are: (800) 523-2929 in the continental United States, Virgin Islands, and Puerto Rico; (800) 462-4983 in Pennsylvania; and (800) 537-4700 in Alaska and Hawaii.

The center has access to a vast computer data base which provides specific types of information from lists of manufacturers of active and passive solar products to state-by-state lists of solar professionals. This information is dis-seminated by computer print-outs. Costs for this service vary and should be checked with the information center. Some lists are free.

The national solar information center also possesses information on educational sources such as training programs, vocational schools and colleges offering degrees in solar technology, and conferences. The listing also includes solar instructional seminars, classes, and correspondence courses.

Another means of instruction is available through films, slides, and tapes on solar energy. These audio-visual materials can be used as a promotional or educational tool for builders and homebuyers. A free catalog is available from the federal solar information center. Some items are loaned free-of-charge. Others cost a nominal fee for rental.

The information center serves as a clearinghouse for solar information from many federal government agencies such as from the *Department of Energy* and the *Department of Housing and Urban Development*. Detailed information on the HUD solar demonstration projects, for example, is available in many different publications. Bibliographies of literature are distributed upon request.

Research reports on energy subjects can be obtained from the *National Technical Information Center*, which is sponsored by the Department of Energy. Publications from NTIC are provided free or at a nominal charge. For more information, contact the National Technical Information Center, Publications Department, P.O. Box 62, Oak Ridge, Tennessee 37830.

Another federal research arm of the Department of Energy is the *Solar Energy Research Institute*. It also disseminates information on solar developments, using a computerized solar information data bank. For more information, contact the Solar Energy Research Institute, 1617 Cole Blvd., Golden, Colorado 80401.

The federal Renewable Energy Information center includes information stored on computers on state solar energy legislation, regulations, and listings of state and private energy organizations. These listings are all available from the information center by phone or letter.

State solar energy centers can provide more specific information on available state incentives, regulations, and in-state solar programs. Information on local, regional, and state-wide solar seminars and conferences is also available from these centers. Many of the state centers can also provide a referral service for builders who have specific technical questions.

State Solar Energy Centers

Alabama Solar Energy Center
Johnson Environmental & Energy Center
University of Alabama/Huntsville
P.O. Box 1247
Huntsville, AL 35807
(205) 895-6361

Alabama Energy Management Board
Rm. 203, Executive Bldg.
312 Montgomery St.
Montgomery, AL 36104
(205) 832-5010

Alaska Dept. of Commerce
Office of Energy Conservation
7th Floor
338 Denali St.
Anchorage, AK 99501
(907) 272-0527

*Toll-free number in state only

Arizona Solar Energy Research Commission
Capital Tower - Rm. 500
1700 W. Washington
Phoenix, AZ 85007
(602) 255-3303

Arkansas Energy Office
960 Plaza West Bldg.
Little Rock, AR 72205
(501) 371-1370

California Energy Commission
1111 Howe Ave.
Sacramento, CA 95825
*(800) 852-7516
 (916) 920-6430

Colorado Office of Energy Conservation
1600 Downing St.
Denver, CO 80218
(303) 839-2507

Connecticut Office of Policy & Management
Energy Division
80 Washington St.
Hartford, CT 06115
*(800) 842-1648
 (203) 566-2800

Delaware Governor's Energy Office
P.O. Box 140
114 W. Water St.
Dover, DE 19901
*(800) 282-8616
 (302) 678-5644

Florida Solar Energy Center
300 State Rd., 401
Cape Canaveral, FL 32920
(305) 783-0300

Florida State Energy Office
301 Bryant Bldg.
Tallahassee, FL 32301
(904) 488-6764

Georgia Office of Energy Resources
Rm. 615
270 Washington St., S.W.
Atlanta, GA 30334
(404) 656-5176

Hawaii State Energy Office
Dept. of Planning & Economic Development
P.O. Box 2359
Honolulu, HI 96804
(808) 548-4150
(808) 548-4080 (on Oahu)
Dial 0 ask for 8016 (toll-free within Hawaii, off
  Oahu)

Idaho State Office of Energy
State House
Boise, ID 83720
(208) 384-3800

Institute of Natural Resources
325 West Adams
Springfield, IL 62706
(217) 782-1926

Indiana Dept. of Commerce
Energy Group
7th Floor-Consolidated Bldg.
115 N. Pennsylvania St.
Indianapolis, IN 46204
(317) 633-6753

Iowa Solar Office
Energy Policy Council
Capitol Complex
Des Moines, IA 50319
(515) 281-8071

State of Kansas Energy Office
Room 241
503 Kansas Ave.
Topeka, KS 66603
*(800) 432-3537
 (913) 296-2496

Kentucky Department of Energy
Capitol Plaza Tower
Frankfort, KY 40601
*(800) 372-7978
 (802) 564-7416

Louisiana Research & Development Division
Dept. of Natural Resources
P.O. Box 44156
Baton Rouge, LA 70804
(504) 342-4594

Maine Office of Energy Resources
55 Capitol St.
Augusta, ME 04330
(207) 289-2195

Maryland Energy Policy Office
Room 1302
301 W. Preston St.
Baltimore, MD 21201
*(800) 494-5903
 (301) 383-6810

Massachusetts Office of Energy Resources
73 Tremont St.
Room 700
Boston, MA 02108
(617) 727-4732

Michigan Energy Administration
Dept. of Commerce
P.O. Box 30228
6520 Mercantile Way, Suite 1
Lansing, MI 48909
*(800) 292-4704
 (517) 374-9090

Minnesota Solar Office
980 American Center Bldg.
150 East Kellog
St. Paul, MN 55101
*(800) 652-9747
 (612) 296-5175

Mississippi Fuel & Energy Management Commission
Suite 228, Barfield Complex
455 North Lamar St.
Jackson, MS 39201
(601) 354-7406

Missouri Dept. of Natural Resources
Division of Policy Development
P.O. Box 1309
Jefferson City, MO 65120
*(800) 392-8269
 (314) 751-4000

Montana Dept. of Natural Resources & Conservation
32 South Ewing
Helena, MT 59601
(406) 449-3940

Nebraska State Solar Office
W-191 Nebraska Hall
University of Nebraska
Lincoln, NE 68588
(402) 472-3414

*Toll-free number in state only

Nebraska State Energy Office
State Capitol
Lincoln, NE 68588
(402) 471-2867

Nevada Dept. of Energy
1050 E. Williams, Suite 405
Capitol Complex
Carson City, NV 89710
(702) 885-5157

New Hampshire Governor's Council on Energy
26 Pleasant St.
Concord, NH 03301
*(800) 562-1115
 (603) 271-2711

New Jersey Office of Alternate Technology
NJ Dept. of Energy
101 Commerce St.
Newark, NJ 07102
*(800) 492-4242
 (201) 648-6293

New Mexico Energy & Minerals Dept.
Energy Conservation & Management Division
P.O. Box 2270
Santa Fe, NM 87501
*(800) 432-6782
 (505) 827-2472
 (505) 827-2386

New York State Energy Office
Agency Building #2
Empire State Plaza
Albany, NY 12223
(518) 474-8181

North Carolina Dept. of Commerce
Energy Division
430 North Salisbury St.
Raleigh, NC 27611
*(800) 662-7131
 (919) 733-2230

North Dakota State Solar Office
1533 N. 12th St.
Bismarck, ND 58501
(701) 224-2250

Ohio Solar Office
30 East Broad St.
34th Floor
Columbus, OH 43215
*(800) 282-9284
 (614) 466-7915

Oklahoma Department of Energy
4400 North Lincoln Boulevard
Suite 251
Oklahoma City, OK 73105
(405) 521-3941

Oregon Dept. of Energy
Rm. 111
Labor & Industries Bldg.
Salem, OR 97310
*(800) 452-7813
 (503) 378-4040

Pennsylvania Governor's Energy Council
1625 N. Front St.
Harrisburg, PA 17102
*(800) 882-8400
 (717) 783-8610

Puerto Rico Office of Energy
Energy Information Program
41089 Minillas Station
Santurce, PR 00940
(809) 727-8877

Rhode Island Governor's Energy Office
80 Dean St.
Providence, RI 02903
(401) 277-3774

South Carolina Energy Management Office
1205 Pendleton St.
Columbia, SC 29201
*(800) 922-1600
 (803) 758-2050

South Dakota State Solar Office
Capital Lake Plaza Bldg.
Pierre, SD 57501
*(800) 592-1865
 (605) 224-3603

Tennessee Energy Authority
707 Capitol Blvd. Bldg.
Nashville, TN 37219
*(800) 642-1340
 (615) 741-2994

*Toll-free number in state only

Texas Office of Energy Resource
7703 North Lamar Street
Austin, TX 78752
(512) 475-5491

Utah Energy Office
231 East 400 South
Empire Building, Suite 101
Salt Lake City, UT 84111
*(800) 662-3633
 (801) 533-5424

Vermont State Energy Office
State Office Bldg.
Montpelier, VT 05602
*(800) 642-3281
 (802) 828-2393

Virginia Division of Energy
310 Turner Street
Richmond, VA 23235
*(800) 552-3831
 (804) 745-3245

Virgin Islands Energy Office
P.O. Box 2996
St. Thomas
U.S. Virgin Islands 00801
(809) 774-6726

Washington State Energy Office
400 East Union St.
1st Floor
Olympia, WA 98504
(206) 754-1370

West Virginia Fuel and Energy Office
1262½ Greenbrier St.
Charleston, WV 25311
*(800) 642-9012
 (304) 348-8860

Wisconsin Division of Energy
1 West Wilson - Rm. 201
Madison, WI 53702
(608) 266-9861

Wyoming Energy Conservation Office
320 West 25th St.
Capital Hill Bldg.
Cheyenne, WY 82001
*(800) 442-6783
 (307) 777-7131

---

*Toll-free number in state only

Two independent associations which sponsor various conferences, exhibits, and other educational opportunities are:

- *Solar Energy Industries Association*, 1001 Connecticut Ave. N.W., Suite 800, Washington D.C. 20036
  (202) 293-2981.
- *American Solar Energy Society*, 1230 Grandview Avenue, Boulder, Colorado 80302
  (303) 492-6017.

State and Regional Chapters of the American Solar Energy Society

Alabama Solar Energy Association
c/o Johnson Environmental & Energy Center
University of Alabama
P.O. Box 1247
Huntsville, AL 35807
(205) 837-4214

Arizona Solar Energy Association
P.O. Box 25396
Phoenix, AZ 85002
(602) 252-0796

Colorado Solar Energy Association
P.O. Box 1284
Alamosa, CO 81101
(303) 589-5184

Eastern New York Solar Energy Assn.
P.O. Box 5181
Albany, NY 12205
(518) 863-4338

Florida Solar Energy Association
P.O. Box 248271
University Station
Miami, FL 33124
(305) 284-3438

Georgia Solar Energy Association
P.O. Box 32748
Atlanta, GA 30332
(404) 894-3636

Hoosier Solar Energy Association
c/o Gordon Clark Associates
611 N. Capitol
Indianapolis, IN 46204
(317) 264-2995

Illinois Solar Energy Association
P.O. Box 1592
Aurora, IL 60507
(312) 886-3320

Iowa Solar Energy Association
P.O. Box 68
Iowa City, IA 52244
(319) 365-6103

Kansas Solar Energy Society
P.O. Box 8516
Wichita, KS 67208
or
c/o Center for Alternate Energies
P.O. Box 1340
Dodge City, KS 67801
(316) 225-0296

Metropolitan NY Solar Energy Society
P.O. Box 2147
Grand Central Station
New York, NY 10163
(914) 725-2249

Michigan Solar Energy Association
c/o Plymouth Library
223 S. Main Street
Plymouth, MI 48170
(313) 459-9420

Mid-Atlantic Solar Energy Assn.
2233 Grays Ferry Avenue
Philadelphia, PA 19146
(215) 545-2150

Minnesota Solar Energy Association
P.O. Box 762
Minneapolis, MN 55440
(612) 535-0305

Mississippi Solar Energy Assn.
225 West Lampkin Road
Starkville, MS 39759
(601) 323-7246

Nebraska Solar Energy Association
c/o University of Nebraska
Engr. Building 261
P.O. Box 688
Omaha, NE 68101
(402) 554-2769

Nevada Solar Advocates
P.O. Box 8179
University Station
Reno, NV 89507
(702) 323-0238

New England Solar Energy Assn.
P.O. Box 541
Brattleboro, VT 05301
(802) 254-2386

New Mexico Solar Energy Assn.
P.O. Box 2004
Santa Fe, NM 87501
(505) 983-2861

North Carolina Solar Energy Assn.
P.O. Box 12235
Research Triangle Park, NC 27709
(919) 821-3591

Northern California Solar Energy Assn.
P.O. Box 886
Berkeley, CA 94701
(415) 843-4306

Ohio Solar Energy Association
c/o Columbus Technical Institute
550 East Spring
Columbus, OH 43215
(614) 227-5005

Oklahoma Solar Energy Association
P.O. Box 2597
Norman, OK 73070
(405) 329-1118

Solar Energy Association of Oregon
c/o Portland SUN
628 SE Mill
Portland, OR 97214
(503) 239-7470

South Dakota Renewable Energy Assn.
P.O. Box 782
Pierre, SD 57501
(605) 224-1115

Tennessee Solar Energy Association
c/o Alternative Energy Farm Project
Route 6, Box 526
Crossville, TN 38555
(615) 788-2736

Texas Solar Energy Society
600 W. 28th, Suite 101
Austin, TX 78705
(512) 472-1252

Virginia Solar Energy Association
c/o Piedmont Technical Associates
300 Lansing Avenue
Lynchburg, VA 24503
(804) 846-0429

Washington Solar Council
1139 34th Avenue
Seattle, WA 98122
(206) 328-0738

Solar Energy Resource Association of Wisconsin
525 University Avenue
Madison, WI 53703
(608) 251-4447

A good source of information about passive solar energy from industry sources is available from the *Passive Solar Industries Council*, c/o Potomac Energy Group, 125 South Royal Street, Alexandria, Virginia 22314. (703) 683-5001.

PSIC also works as a lobby group in Washington, D.C. Another political group is the *Solar Lobby*, 1001 Connecticut Ave. N.W., Washington, D.C. 20036, (202) 466-6350. It monitors legislation in Washington, D.C. and encourages support of solar causes on a grassroots level.

Other industry groups, manufacturers, universities and colleges, and home builders associations also sponsor educational programs and offer publications. While they can answer general or technical questions, they may also be able to provide references to qualified solar professional individuals or groups.

SUBJECT INDEX

C

California, 76–77, 116–121, 126–127, 154–157, 167–178, 191–194

Ceiling fan, 13, 37, 85–86, 193–194 (see also Ventilation)

Chimney effect, 18–19, 65, 130

Clerestory windows, 85–86

Climatic zones, 139 (see also Northern climates and Southern climates)

Code officials, 126, 165–166

Collectors, 3–4
  efficiency, 6, 69
  hiding from view, 73, 76–77
  number needed, 5
  on-site fabrication, 73, 75
  orientation, 4, 11, 126–127
  remote arrays, 50, 155, 174
  schematic, 3
  tubular, 59

Colorado, 31–46, 80, 106, 113–116, 184–188
  Office of Energy Conservation, 31, 196

Computer
  calculations, 96
  home systems, 49–50, 119–120
  storage of solar data, 195 (see also Monitoring performance)

Connecticut, 47–50, 94–96, 182–184

Conservation and Renewable Energy Inquiry and Referral Service, 195

Construction steps, 115, 186–187

Consumer attitudes, 64, 67, 109–112, 140, 178

Convection, 13, 18–19, 65, 130, 142–144, 148, 190 (see also Ventilation, natural)

Copper Development Association, 47–50

Corporate solar task force, 174

Cost analysis, 138

Cost-effective design and construction, 94–96, 119, 121, 137–159, 174–175, 190

Cost of solar systems and components, 8, 27–28, 31, 53–54, 58, 64–65, 69, 78, 83, 86–88, 92, 94, 96–97, 110, 114, 116, 121, 126, 128, 130, 137–140, 144–145, 147, 149, 153–154, 159, 178, 184, 190–192

Crawl spaces and basements, 18–19, 62–63, 130

D

Demonstration programs, 22–69, 151–154 (see also Department of Housing and Urban Development, residential solar grant program)
  demonstration house, 97–100

Department of Energy, 11, 30–31, 64–65, 88, 165–166, 195

Department of Housing and Urban Development, 3, 6, 8, 12, 111–112, 195
  residential solar grant program, 25–31, 67, 78, 82–83, 109–115, 165, 178, 185

Direct gain, 12–13, 15, 33, 40, 46, 74, 85, 89, 93, 119, 128, 152

Ductwork and piping, 8, 73, 115, 179, 185

E

Eaves, solar control, 19 (see also Overhangs)

Economical feasibility, 28–29, 137, 163

Educational seminars, 32, 114, 154, 178, 195

Energy-efficient construction, 3, 8, 15, 16, 67, 73, 87, 94, 109, 124, 133, 140–141, 163, 167, 180, 182, 192

Energy-saving components, 49, 65, 96, 116, 138, 141, 151, 182, 184 (see also Passive solar components)

Envelope house, 130

Eutectic salts, 65 (see also Heat pumps)

Experimental programs, 47–65
  prototype homes, 153–154

F

Family Circle magazine, 100, 149

Farmers Home Administration, mortgage program, 154

Federal Energy Administration, 4, 7

Federal Housing Authority, insured mortgage program, 121, 140, 154, 175

Flip-flop plans, 37 (see also Land planning)

G

General Accounting Office, study, 29

Georgia, 97–100

Glazing, 14–15, 33, 40, 46, 56–57, 65, 89, 100, 123, 144, 174 (see also Window placement)

Greenhouse, 12–13, 19, 45, 47, 52–53, 55, 88, 90–91, 130–133, 191 (see also Sunspace)

H

Heat distribution, 11–12, 88, 97, 103, 105, 115, 119, 123, 148–149, 190

Heat loss, reduction of, 13, 15, 20, 35, 39, 50, 57, 128

Heat pumps (see also Back-up heat)
  air-to-air, 49, 105
  conventional, 100, 149

NAME INDEX